ARKANSAS GUIDE TO EXECUTIVE CLEMENCY

including Arkansas Parole Board Policy Manual
(Second Edition)

by
John Wesley Hall

Criminal Defense Lawyer
Past President, National Association of Criminal Defense Lawyers
Fellow, American Board of Criminal Lawyers
Best Lawyers in America, Criminal Defense &
White Collar Criminal Defense

1202 Main Street, Suite 210
Little Rock, Arkansas 72202
501-371-9131
hall@forhall.com

www.JohnWesleyHall.com
www.FourthAmendment.com

Disclaimer

This book is current as of its publication in January 2014, and it should be current for at least the year 2014. New forms and policies came from the Parole Board in late 2013. Remember that forms and policies can change at any time, and a new Governor takes office January 15, 2015.

You should get forms from the prison librarian or Institutional Parole Office. If you are not in prison, they can be printed off the Parole Board's website: http://paroleboard.arkansas.gov (under the Executive Clemency tab). If later forms are published, they control over what is reproduced in the Appendices.

This information is general in nature and should never be relied on as a substitute for legal advice for your specific situation.

FOREWORD

This book is written for the benefit of persons convicted in Arkansas and their loved ones who are trying to get them out of prison early by a time cut or get their records cleared by a pardon.

You do not need a lawyer to do a clemency or pardon petition.[1] The Governor's Office reports that persons who file their own clemency requests, if they are clearly and well presented, usually do as well before the Parole Board and Governor as those represented by lawyers.

If your case is factually complicated, you should seriously consider hiring a lawyer to prepare and present the petition for you. Two examples:

In the early 1990's we had a clemency petition based on newly discovered evidence and an unreasonable sentence from a jury. Our preparation included spending nearly a week in the Circuit Clerk's Office analyzing all sentences for similar crimes for five years before and after the inmate's trial. We also had reports of experts and investigators showing the newly-discovered evidence, and we analyzed how it made the prosecution case less believable. The application with attachments was about 3,000 pages long. The sentence was reduced from life to a term of years, and the inmate was later paroled. Few cases are as complicated as that one.

About 2004, we did a clemency for an inmate who insisted on a jury trial in a drug case and got a good outcome from the jury with a minimum sentence on the counts he was convicted on. The jury recommended concurrent sentences, but the Circuit Judge made the sentences consecutive (10 x 4), which was his legal right. The Parole Board recommended clemency, and the Governor granted it. The inmate still served twice as long as the jury's recommendation, but half of what the judge imposed. (Sometimes it is better to have taken the deal in court because you can

---

[1] Watch out for lawyers who claim to have special influence with the Governor or Parole Board to get you clemency. Such claims by lawyers are unethical and unlawful; Ark. Rules of Professional Conduct 8.4(e); and the Parole Board and Governor would not be influenced anyway. Also, there is too much public scrutiny in the clemency and pardon process. (*See also* § 3)

never count on clemency.)

These are just examples, and your case probably will be different.

"Time cuts" are hard to get. At the time this is written, Governor Beebe has granted only seven "time cuts" out of probably 1,000 submitted.[2] This likely will remain that way for a really long time, past the terms of Governor Beebe which ends January 15, 2015. Remember, as stated in § 2, executive clemency is purely a matter of discretion with the Governor, and it is not subject to review by anybody.

J.W.H.
January 2014

---

[2] As of the time this was published.

TABLE OF CONTENTS

§ 1.   Introduction.. 1
§ 2.   The executive power of the Governor 2
§ 3.   Statutory regulation of pardon and executive clemency.. 3
§ 4.   Parole Board regulations ("Policy Manual"). 3
§ 5.   Grounds for executive clemency. 4
§ 6.   To correct an injustice which may have occurred during the person's
            trial.. 5
§ 7.   The inmate has a life-threatening medical condition 6
§ 8.   To reduce an excessive sentence 8
§ 9.   The person's institutional adjustment has been exemplary, and the
            ends of justice have been achieved. 9
§ 10.   When to apply 10
§ 11.   The form.. 10
§ 12.   Content of the form.. 11
§ 13.   Attachments and letters.. 11
§ 14.   "Explain why you think the Governor should grant you a commutation
            (time cut)". 12
§ 15.   Be absolutely candid, truthful, and complete in the paperwork; you
            are under oath. 12
§ 16.   Filing the request. 14
§ 17.   Clemency papers as public records.. 14
§ 18.   Parole Board hearing. 15
§ 19.   How long does it take?. 16
§ 20.   If denied, what then?.. 17
§ 21.   Pardon requests.. 17
§ 22.   Sealing of pardoned offenses. 20
§ 23.   Relief from firearms disabilities (prohibitions). 20
§ 24.   Death penalty clemencies.. 20

Appendices
        A   Arkansas Board of Parole Policy Manual (revised September
                26, 2013)
        B   Statutes Governing Pardon and Clemency
        C   Executive Clemency ("Time Cut") Forms
        D   Pardon Forms

§ 1. Introduction

Executive clemency means two things: a "time cut" or a pardon. From the Arkansas Parole Board's website:

> A **pardon** is a total forgiveness of a criminal penalty.[3]
>
> . . .
>
> A **commutation** is a reduction of a criminal penalty.

If a "time cut" is granted by the Governor, you would get out of prison early. Since 2007, they have been rare under Governor Beebe, and less than 1% have been granted.[4] Whether that will change with the Governor in office from January 2015–January 2019 is completely unknown. Don't expect it to change.

A pardon may be granted by the Governor if the applicant has shown a positive adjustment to life, school, work, family, and society in general. Pardons should almost always be filed well after release from prison.

A pardon is a restoration of civil rights, but a "time cut" is not. (*See* § 23)

This book primarily focuses on executive clemency ("time cut"), but the same considerations in preparing the paperwork usually apply to both clemency and pardons.

The Appendices to this book include:

> A. The ARKANSAS PAROLE BOARD POLICY MANUAL (rev. September 26, 2013) (referred to as the "Policy Manual"),[5] and the most pertinent pages are 19–22 & 30;
>
> B. Four statutes governing clemency in Arkansas;

---

[3] It may be "forgiveness," but it doesn't disappear from a criminal history available to law enforcement and licensing agencies. *See* § 22.

[4] *See* Foreword at ii.

[5] In the first edition, only the pertinent pages of the Policy Manual were included. Now the entire Policy Manual is included.

C.   The Parole Board's clemency form; and

D.   The Parole Board's pardon form.

§ 2.   The Executive Power of the Governor

Pardon or clemency is an act of grace from the government to the individual. It is an executive decision by the Governor,[6] and it is not subject to any judicial review under separation of powers.

The power to grant a pardon or grant executive clemency rests solely with the Governor, subject to reasonable regulation, but not limits, by the legislature.[7]

Nearly all chief executives have the power to grant pardons and executive clemency. Arkansas has had such power since statehood. In the current 1874

---

[6] See, e.g., *Nelson v. Hall,* 171 Ark. 683, 687, 285 S.W. 386, 387 (1926):

> A pardon by the sovereign from the effects of conviction of crime has always been regarded as purely an act of grace. Chief Justice Marshall, in the case of *United States v. Wilson,* 32 U.S. 150, 7 Peters 160, defined a pardon as "an act of grace proceeding from the power intrusted with the execution of the law." This is the substance of every definition given of the exercise of the pardoning power. The merits of the applicant do not in any sense afford a consideration to justify a reformation of the instrument to cure defects, nor do the circumstances of a particular case have the effect of introducing the element of contract into the execution of the instrument, but those circumstances merely appeal to the executive in determining whether or not clemency should be extended. After all, and regardless of the reasons which appeal to the executive, his act in extending clemency is merely one of grace—a gratuity—a favor which may be arbitrarily extended or withheld.

Baldwin v. Scoggin, 15 Ark. 427, 433 (1855) ("necessary and humane prerogative, conferred upon him by the Constitution.")

[7] See *Horton v. Gillespie,* 170 Ark. 107, 113-14, 279 S.W. 1020, 1022 (1926), on the power of the legislature to regulate.

constitution, it is in Ark. Const., art. 6, § 18:

> In all criminal and penal cases, except in those of treason and impeachment, the Governor shall have power to grant reprieves, commutations of sentence, and pardons, after conviction; and to remit fines and forfeitures, under such rules and regulations as shall be prescribed by law. . . . He shall communicate to the General Assembly at every regular session each case of reprieve, commutation or pardon, with his reasons therefor; stating the name and crime of the convict, the sentence, its date, and the date of the commutation, pardon or reprieve.

§ 3. Statutory regulation of pardon and executive clemency

Pardon and executive clemency are also subject to limited regulated by statute. They are Ark. Code Ann. §§ 5-4-607, 16-93-204, 16-93-207, and 16-90-1411 in Appendix B, below. There are other statutes quoted in the footnotes. Another applies only in death penalty cases.

The purpose of statutory regulation of the pardon and clemency power is to make known any abuse of power by the Governor in a clemency or pardon which last allegedly happened in 1993 by the President pro tem of the Senate when the Governor was out-of-state.[8]

§ 4. Parole Board regulations ("Policy Manual")

The Parole Board also has regulations which govern how clemency is processed and heard by the Board. They are in the Policy Manual at pp. 19-22, 30 in Appendix A.

The Parole Board is a part of the executive branch of government, and it is appropriate for the Governor to delegate to the Parole Board the investigative and

---

[8] *See Baldwin v. Scoggin,* 15 Ark. 427, 433 (1855).

In 1993, there briefly was no Lt. Governor after Governor Clinton resigned to become President of the United States, and the Governor was in Washington for the Inauguration.

screening function of the parole process. The Parole Board's favorable recommendation is not executive clemency, and its vote creates no rights to clemency or a pardon because that is the Governor's power alone.[9]

Similarly, the Parole Board's finding of "without merit" is not binding on the Governor, and, in pardon applications, past Governors have granted pardons that the Parole Board thought were "without merit."

§ 5. Grounds for executive clemency

The grounds recognized for a grant of executive clemency or a pardon (Policy Manual at p. 20, § 4.3) are:

1.   To correct an injustice which may have occurred during the person's trial (*see* Ark. Code Ann. § 16-93-207(c)(3)(A)(ii) recognizing newly discovered evidence or other "meritorious circumstances")
2.   The inmate has a life-threatening medical condition (*also see id.* & Ark. Code Ann. § 12-29-404;)
3.   To reduce an excessive sentence;
4.   The person's institutional adjustment has been exemplary, and the

---

[9] *Smith v. Huckabee,* 2007 Ark. LEXIS 188 (Mar. 7, 2007) (unpublished), rehearing denied, 2007 Ark. LEXIS 247 (Apr. 12, 2007) (unpublished):

Moreover, any limitations on the governor's discretion would conflict with the exclusive power granted that executive officer under Ark. Const. art. 6, § 18. Under our constitution, the executive branch has sole authority to grant clemency. *Coones v. State,* 280 Ark. 321, 657 S.W.2d 553 (1983) (citing *Smith v. State,* 262 Ark. 239, 555 S.W.2d 569 (1977)). Legislative action cannot override constitutional provisions. *Abbott v. State,* 256 Ark. 558, 508 S.W.2d 733 (1974). Appellant did not point to any other statute that might have application to a request for clemency and the governor is not required to follow any statute in determining whether to grant a request for clemency. Appellant's due-process argument also fails under this analysis, as there are no constraints in the statute, or any statute, that the governor failed to follow.

ends of justice have been achieved.

§ 6. To correct an injustice which may have occurred during the person's trial

Under Arkansas law, newly-discovered evidence that comes too late to be used in court or included in a petition in court can still be used for a pardon or clemency.[10] In *Williams v. Langston,* the Arkansas Supreme Court said in 1985:

> Once a conviction has been affirmed on appeal, error coram nobis is not available to secure a new trial on the basis of newly discovered evidence or to raise issues which are properly raised in a petition pursuant to Criminal Procedure Rule 37. *See Pickens v. State,* 284 Ark. 506, 683 S.W.2d 614 (1985); see also *Penn v. State,* 282 Ark. 571, 670 S.W.2d 426 (1984). If a petitioner discovers some ground for relief such as that claimed by the petitioner in *Pickens* after a judgment is affirmed, he may present that ground in a clemency proceeding.[11]

There is a court mechanism in Arkansas law for presenting newly-developed scientific evidence in some cases[12] and writ of error coram nobis for other newly discovered evidence that would affect the outcome.[13] If it fails in court, however, it could still be an available ground for clemency.

> Where there was no fundamental error at the time of trial, newly discovered evidence is not a cause to issue a writ of error coram

---

[10] *Brown v. State,* 330 Ark. 627, 632, 955 S.W.2d 901, 903 (1997) ("Assertions of a third-party confession after a judgment is affirmed may be addressed to the executive branch in a clemency proceeding.").

[11] 285 Ark. 444, 445, 688 S.W.2d 285, 286 (1985).

[12] 2001 Ark. Act 1780, as amended; Ark. Code Ann. § 16-112-201 *et seq.*

[13] *Larimore v. State,* 327 Ark. 271, 279-80, 938 S.W.2d 818, 822 (1997) (the fact that evidence is "newly discovered" is not enough; it must create a fundamental error with the trial).

nobis. *Smith v. State, supra.* The mere fact that over time a scientific test may have been developed which did not exist at the time of a petitioner's trial is not in itself cause to issue the writ because the development in scientific testing cannot establish a fundamental error made at trial. A petitioner who contends that newly developed scientific testing can exonerate him should submit the allegation to the executive branch in a clemency proceeding.[14]

This is now also recognized in Ark. Code Ann. § 16-93-207(c)(3)(A)(ii)(a, c) (App. B).

The harshness of statute is also consideration in granting clemency.[15]

I do not think that filing a clemency from a guilty or no contest plea is barred, if you can truly show injustice that affected the sentence or maybe even the plea. Remember, however, a guilty plea is weighty evidence, and it is hard to argue that a bargained for sentence in a guilty plea is ever excessive, but it can be and has been done where the facts were compelling, such as where similarly situated co-defendants or even defendants in other cases were treated differently.

§ 7. The inmate has a life-threatening medical condition

An inmate may gain release by clemency if a prison and a community doctor believe that the inmate is terminal and will die within a year. Medical records would have to be made available. Parole for a terminal medical condition, however, is faster for everybody concerned. Ark. Code Ann. § 12-29-404(b)(2) ("Act 290" as amended):

> (a) As used in this section:
>> (1) "Permanently incapacitated" means, as determined by a licensed physician, that an inmate:
>>> (A) Has a medical condition that is not necessar-

---

[14] *Pitts v. State,* 336 Ark. 580, 584, 986 S.W.2d 407, 409-10 (1999).

[15] *Alexander v. State,* 77 Ark. 294, 299, 91 S.W. 181, 182 (1905) ("These facts would doubtless appeal with much force for executive clemency, but afford no ground for relief in the courts, where the law must be enforced as it is written.").

ily terminal but renders him or her permanently and irreversibly incapacitated; and

      (B) Requires immediate and long-term care; and

    (2) "Terminally ill" means, as determined by a licensed physician, that an inmate:

      (A) Has an incurable condition caused by illness or disease; and

      (B) Will likely die within two (2) years due to the illness or disease.

(b) The Director of the Department of Correction or the Director of the Department of Community Correction[16] shall communicate to the Parole Board when, in the independent opinions of either a Department of Correction physician or Department of Community Correction physician and a consultant physician in Arkansas, an inmate is either terminally ill or permanently incapacitated and should be considered for transfer to parole supervision.

(c)   (1) Upon receipt of a communication described in subsection (b) of this section, the board shall assemble or request all such information as is germane to determine whether the inmate is eligible under this section for immediate transfer to parole supervision.

    (2) If the facts warrant and the board is satisfied that the inmate's physical condition makes the inmate no longer a threat to public safety, the board may approve the inmate for immediate transfer to parole supervision.

(d) An inmate is not eligible for parole supervision under this section if he or she is required to register as a sex offender under the Sex Offender Registration Act of 1997, § 12-12-901 et seq., and:

    (1) The inmate is assessed as a Level 3 offender or higher; or

    (2) A victim of one (1) or more of the inmate's sex offenses was fourteen (14) years of age or younger.

(e) The board may revoke a person's parole supervision granted under this section if the person's medical condition improves to the point that he or she would initially not have been eligible for parole

---

[16] Now called "Arkansas Community Correction."

supervision under this section.

See also Ark. Code Ann. § 16-93-207(c)(3)(A)(ii)(b) (App. B.)

§ 8.   To reduce an excessive sentence

Arkansas is a jury sentencing state.[17] An overly long jury sentence in any case in Arkansas is always a ground for executive clemency. The Parole Board and Governor both recognize it, and it is one of the things clemency is for in a jury sentencing state. What, however, is an overly long sentence? It depends on many factors, and no two cases are alike.

Any sentence within the statutory range of punishment is legally and presumptively reasonable.[18] And, once a judgment and commitment or sentencing order has been signed by the Circuit Judge and the sentence has been put into effect, it cannot be amended or modified by the courts.[19]

An illegal sentence may be corrected at any time, including on appeal, such as where the statutory maximum is 40 years and the court imposes 50. That is done by a state habeas corpus petition for a facially illegal sentence.

A federal habeas case in Arkansas granted relief where the Eighth Circuit found a life sentence given by a jury for delivery of .238 grams of crack was cruel and unusual punishment in violation of the Eighth Amendment. The U.S. Sentencing Guidelines for the same offense in federal court was 10-16 months.[20]

If a sentence is unreasonable under the facts of the case, that would be a

---

[17]   There are only four jury sentencing states left.

[18]   *Buckley v. State,* 349 Ark. 53, 64, 76 S.W.3d 825, 832 (2002).

[19]   *Redding v. State,* 293 Ark. 411, 413, 738 S.W.2d 410, 411 (1987) ("After the sentence is put into execution the power to change the sentence passes from the trial court to the executive branch of government. *Nelson v. State,* 284 Ark. 156, 680 S.W.2d 91 (1984).").

[20]   *Henderson v. Norris,* 258 F.3d 706 (8th Cir. 2001).

ground for executive clemency—it is not a question for the courts.[21] That is a part of the historical function of clemency because Arkansas is a jury sentencing state, and juries can sentence defendants to completely arbitrary sentences. It happens every day. The same case in different counties can produce vastly different sentences.

A high sentence alone most likely will not work to get a "time cut" in a violent or sex crime, but it might very well in a drug or property crime where the inmate has no or very few priors. Life imprisonment from a jury verdict where the same prosecutor was pleading people to, for example, 20 years, would show valid reason for clemency because the lifer was penalized for asserting his constitutional right to a jury trial.[22] The right to a jury trial cannot constitutionally be punished when others are pleading for much less.[23]

In the Foreword, I talked about cases where we were successful. In those cases, however, the inmates still served a lot longer than those who pled, even though they were granted clemency to reduce their sentence.

§ 9. The person's institutional adjustment has been exemplary, and the ends of justice have been achieved.

If the inmate has an excellent prison disciplinary record, and has attended all the classes available, the inmate can apply on the ground that "[t]he person's institutional adjustment has been exemplary, and the ends of justice have been achieved."

This enables virtually anybody to apply, but it should be cautioned that

---

[21] *Jamett v. State*, 2010 Ark. 28 at 7 ("Any claim of prejudice based on the severity of the sentence is an issue for a plea for executive clemency and is unavailing in a Rule 37.1 petition."); *Pettit v. State,* 296 Ark. 423, 431, 758 S.W.2d 1, 5 (1988); *Rogers v. State,* 265 Ark. 945, 961-62, 582 S.W.2d 7, 15 (1979); *Smith v. State,* 262 Ark. 239, 240, 555 S.W.2d 569, 570 (1977).

[22] *See* the example in Foreword at i.

[23] Even a high fine can be eliminated by clemency. *Fischel v. Mills,* 55 Ark. 344, 346, 18 S.W. 237, 237 (1892); *Baldwin v. Scoggin,* 15 Ark. 427, 433-34 (1855).

merely telling the Parole Board that "I'm ready to go home" almost certainly carries no weight with them because everybody in prison is "ready to go home." I've had clients say this repeatedly, and it never worked. They had to have some other good reason, too.

Where the sentences have been completed, the Governor has granted many pardons where the applicant shows that they have progressed with school, work, and life in general.

The current Governor has, however, only commuted seven sentences since he took office in January 2007. One was because a black co-defendant of a white inmate received a longer sentence, and the difference could not be justified.

§ 10. When to apply?

The current version of the clemency form (Appendix C) does not have any time limits. Much earlier versions of the clemency form did on the "Reasons" page, but that rule has not been followed for a long time.

A lot of factors bear on when a clemency application should be filed. Foremost should be when you have put together a good enough "case" to make to the Parole Board that you fit in one of the above four categories. The former Policy Manual said that once an application has been filed, it could not be withdrawn or changed without starting the process all over again. The current Policy Manual does not say that.

If you are on parole or probation, the Governor's Office prefers you be "off paper" when you apply.

Important: If you file too soon and clemency is denied by the Governor, you will have to wait four, six or eight years to reapply (§ 20). It is better to wait until you are *really* ready and all your materials are ready to submit with it.

§ 11. The forms

The current version of the clemency and pardon forms are available at the Arkansas Parole Boards website: http://paroleboard.arkansas.gov (under the Executive Clemency tab). They are reproduced in Appendices C–D. Make sure you have the most recent form, just in case.

If you are an inmate in the Arkansas Department of Correction, you can get the form from the Institutional Release Office (IRO) at your unit.

The form says to print or type the application using blue or black ink. Few people have typewriters anymore, and, for our use, we have converted the forms to a word processing document that looks like the original. The Parole Board and the Governor's Office will accept forms like that, although the IRO's have attempted to reject computer prepared forms in the past.

§ 12. Content of the forms; attachments and letters

The form should be as complete as possible. **Every section must be filled out. If a section is not applicable, then write "not applicable" or "none" there.** Some places in the forms will not give you enough room to say all you need to say. Use additional sheets, and say something like "continued on page __" or "attached as Exhibit A".

Note that Reason 1, "injustice," on the clemency form, § 6, above, says "an injustice which may have occurred during the *trial*." Filing a clemency from a guilty or no contest plea is not barred, *if* you can show an "injustice" in your case, but it will be harder to persuade anybody that your sentence should be cut. It has been done, but not recently, and it's just not easy.

If you pled guilty, actual innocence will be hard to show the Parole Board and Governor for clemency or a pardon, but it too can be done. Even innocent people have pled guilty or no contest to cut their losses.

§ 13. Attachments and letters

Under Reason 1, it says "I have attached letters or other documentation that will support this claim. (If you wish to attach explanations or statements to this application, it will be considered as a part of the application.)" These letters are important. They should come from people who know you and your family, and they should be honest and from the heart. You and your family can always get people to write letters saying good things, but read them carefully before you submit them to the Parole Board. Do you really want this person's statement included? Is the statement honest about you and your crime? You must also assume that the letter writer will be contacted for their real opinion, which may be different.

Reason 2 on "terminal medical condition," § 7, requires medical reports be attached. Reason 3 on "excessive sentence" will require you to show why. The fact you don't like it probably isn't enough. Even Reason 4 on "exemplary institutional record" and "ends of justice being achieved" would allow attachments. The Parole Board will have your complete inmate file (your "jacket") with all your disciplinary actions–so you do not need to include that. If you have a disciplinary record, own up to it. They will have it in front of them, so you need to explain. And don't rationalize your past misconduct in prison. You have to own up to it and show that you are a better person now.

§ 14. "Explain why you think the Governor should grant you a commutation (time cut)"

Section 5 on page 7 of the clemency form is important: "Explain why you think the Governor should grant you a commutation (time cut)." This and the following section 5 on describing your rehabilitation are highly important parts of the form. Here, you get to say in your own words why you should have your time cut, and it must be from the heart and not contrived.

Thousands of requests for time cuts have been made to the Parole Board and Governor. What can you say about yourself, your crime, and your rehabilitation that makes you worthy of getting released early?

§ 15. Be absolutely candid, truthful, and complete in the paperwork; you are under oath

As the form states: **Incorrect information will be grounds for denial.** Clemency Form at 1 (App. C).

Be absolutely candid, truthful, and complete in the paperwork. *You cannot and should not attempt to hide anything.* They will find out the whole truth, and you will be hurt by hiding any facts. Even if they don't reject it for that reason, your application loses all its credibility. If you weren't candid about one thing, why should they believe the rest of it?

Being completely truthful about what got you convicted and taking responsibility for your actions is important to those reviewing your request. Your form will be read by a lot of people, and all the factual claims you make will be checked out. (Policy Manual at pp. 21, § 4.6) If your criminal history is incomplete, they will know it, and that will get you denied. If you falsify or unduly mitigate your role in the crime contrary to the jury verdict or the statement at the time of the plea, they will know it because somebody else will point it out. You cannot expect to put anything over on them, so don't even try.

It is imperative that you be absolutely candid and truthful in a clemency or pardon application. If you did something wrong, you have to admit it. You did, after all, get convicted. If you don't take responsibility for what you did, the Parole Board and Governor will readily see it, and they could, and probably would, deny the request on that ground alone. They don't even have to tell you why it was "without merit." And, if it was denied for any reason, you have to wait a long time to refile (§ 20).

Aside from the importance of being candid, the form must be signed under oath, and it is subject to the penalties of perjury if it is false.[24] Remember this at the bottom of the form on page 7 over the signature line, in bold face:

By signing and submitting this application, I hereby swear and affirm that the information provided is true and accurate to the best of my knowledge and I hereby waive any state or federal privacy protections or other privileges to the extent allowable by law.

I understand that incorrect information provided, will be grounds for IMMEDIATE DENIAL!

They mean it, and it only makes sense. Absolute candor and honestly and acceptance of responsibility is required.

------

[24] Maybe you think they will not bother to prosecute for perjury because you are already doing time. Don't count on it. Furthermore, if you get caught in lies, a later clemency application will not be believed.

§ 16. Filing the request

If you are in custody, the completed form with attachments are filed with the IRO at the unit.

If the form is filed from outside the prison it goes to:

> DCC Institutional Release Services (IRS)
> Executive Clemency Department
> 2801 S. Olive St. Suite 6-D
> Pine Bluff, AR 71603

Only the original needs to be filed.

Do not file it with the Parole Board or the Governor. Some family members do this, and it will delay things because the Parole Board and Governor cannot accept the filings. The application has to be screened first by the Parole Board which has a mechanism for doing it.

§ 17. Clemency papers as public records

As I said above, a lot of people will see your application. As it moves through the system, it is entirely possible, even likely, it will be shown to others in the criminal justice system outside the Parole Board. That is another reason to be candid, truthful, and complete. You should assume that the Prosecuting Attorney who prosecuted you will likely see it, and he or she will be able to comment and make a recommendation on grant or denial, and they will surely notice facts you withheld if you aren't candid. *See* Policy Manual at p. 24, § 5.5:

> **Inspection of Records**
>
> The Board of Parole staff will not release information to inmates or the public unless authorized in this manual or in writing by the Board Chairperson. All requests for information should be forwarded to the Department of Community Correction Public Relations Office.
>
> Parole and Executive Clemency Files – Pursuant to the provisions of Ark. Code Ann. § 16-93-202, the following portions of Parole and

Clemency files will be provided by the DCC Public Relations Office for inspection upon request by a person having a proper interest therein and whenever the interests or welfare of the person involved make inspection desirable or helpful: 153 forms, Executive Clemency (commutation & pardon) and vote worksheets. The Public Relations Office may release other information unless restricted by law. The Board Chairperson or Public Relations Office may release information to researchers and others involved in monitoring or studying the criminal justice system unless restricted by law.

Also, it is probable that any clemency application is a public record under the Arkansas Freedom of Information Act,[25] so anybody can see it.

§ 18. Parole Board hearing

The Parole Board is not obligated to hold a hearing. *See* Policy Manual at p. 21, § 4.7:

An applicant for executive clemency who appears before the Board may be accompanied by supporters, including his/her attorney. If the person is not incarcerated in this state, his/her appearance before the Board is not necessary. The Board shall consider the statements of the applicant and a spokesperson, the applicant's file, reports from law enforcement, a presentence report and any documentary evidence presented by the applicant or other interested persons, including the victim(s) (or the victim(s)' next-of-kin). On the basis of this information, the Board will vote (1) to recommend that clemency be granted, or (2) to recommend that clemency be denied. If the Board recommends that clemency be granted, it may specify the nature and terms of the commutation being recommended.

Denial of a hearing does not mean that the application has been determined by them to be "without merit."

If you have a hearing, it will be at your prison unit, and you can have friends,

---

[25] Ark. Code Ann. § 25-19-101 *et seq.*

15

supporters, and a lawyer show up to speak for you. They are scheduled on regular parole hearing days, about once a month. Your hearing won't be held for a few months after you file it to allow time for a preliminary investigation.

The Parole Board member conducting your hearing will give you all the time you really need, but, if you waste time or start repeating yourself, you will be cut off, and you should be. Do not waste their time so they will listen to all you have to say. Be focused in what you and your supporters have to say. Plan for and practice what you will say.

They hold these hearings on regular Parole Hearing dates at the unit, and they have a lot of people to see besides you.

§ 19. How long does it take?

The entire clemency process takes about a year. There is a 30-day waiting period at the beginning and end of the process. After your application is investigated by the Parole Board (which can subpoena records[26]), a hearing may be set where one or two members of the Board will interview the inmate, the inmate's lawyer, and any other people you bring in for support.

Then the victims and the Prosecuting Attorney and police involved with your case have a chance to be heard, but not at the prison and not in your presence. You do not speak in front of them, either.

After the Governor gets it, he has 240 days to study it. The Governor can act at any time during that period.

If granted, you can be released on parole when your new release date comes. You will remain a felon subject to all firearms disabilities (prohibitions) unless you are pardoned or get a specific release from firearms disabilities from the Governor. (§ 22)

In a death penalty case seeking clemency to life without parole, it takes 40 days because only a commutation is sought and an execution date is looming. These

---

[26] Ark. Code Ann. § 16-93-207(c).

are always presented by lawyers for the inmate, and they are beyond the scope of what you need to know for your petition.

§ 20.   If denied, what then?

The Parole Board makes a recommendation to the Governor: "with merit" or "without merit."[27]   The Parole Board's recommendation is not binding on the Governor; it is the Governor's decision, not theirs.

If the Governor takes **no action**, your petition is not granted, but you can reapply any time.

If the Governor **denies** clemency, you cannot reapply for four years from the date of the *application*. If, however, you are doing life for a crime other than Capital Murder, and you are denied, you cannot reapply for six years from the date of the *denial*. If you are doing life without parole for a conviction of Capital Murder, you will not be eligible to reapply for eight years from the date of the *denial*.

There is no appeal from a denial of clemency. The Arkansas Constitution (§ 2) vests this power solely in the Governor and, under separation of powers, the courts have no power to say whether it was done rightly or wrongly.

§ 21. Pardon requests

In Arkansas, a pardon is defined as "an act of grace, proceeding from the power entrusted with the execution of the laws."[28] Pardons can be granted for any reason, or no reason.

> Generally speaking, the pardoning power is to be exercised on
> the ground that the public welfare will be as well promoted by suspen-

---

[27] The Parole Board's actions on clemencies since 2012 are posted on the Arkansas Parole Board website: http://paroleboard.arkansas.gov (under Executive Clemency tab).

[28] *Dover v. Bickle,* 171 Ark. 683, 285 S.W. 386, 388 (1926), quoting *United States v. Wilson,* 32 U.S. 150, 160 (1833) (and pardons may be conditional).

sion as by execution of the sentence; and the power may also be used to correct injustice; but the granting of a pardon is purely discretionary and not a matter of right.

The pardoning power is founded on considerations of the public good, and is to be exercised on the ground that the public welfare, which is the legitimate object of all punishment, will be as well promoted by a suspension as by an execution of the sentence. It may also be used to the end that justice be done by correcting injustice, as where after–discovered facts convince the official or board invested with the power that there was no guilt or that other mistakes were made in the operation or enforcement of the criminal law. Executive clemency also exists to afford relief from undue harshness or evident mistake in the operation or enforcement of the criminal law.

A pardon is granted, not as a matter of right, but as a matter of grace bestowed by the government through its duly authorized officers or departments. It is not, however, a personal favor or a private act of grace from the individual happening to possess power; it is granted as an act in the interest of the public welfare. The exercise of the power lies in the absolute and uncontrolled discretion of the officer in whom it is vested. An executive may grant or deny a pardon for good reasons or bad, or for any reason at all, and such an act is final and irrevocable. . . . The chief executive, acting for the public welfare and the benefit of convict, has the complete discretion in exercising any power of clemency and may exercise the power for whatever reasons he or she thinks appropriate.[29]

Pardon requests by inmates are rarely granted. The inmate should to seek a "time cut" first. After release from prison, you can always file for a pardon when the time is right.

First time pardon applicants have to submit a copy of:

1.   the Judgment and Commitment Order or Sentencing Order from the issuing Circuit Court or District Court,

2.   any probable cause statement in the clerk's file, and

---

[29] C.J.S. *Pardon* § 11.

3. the police narrative file from the arresting agency.

Your discovery packet from your lawyer should have (2) and (3) in it.

Depending on your situation, pardon applications can be simple or complicated. Complicated ones can include recommendation letters and attachments as in clemency requests. (*See* § 13) Simple ones are many of those granted 20 or more years after conviction for a non-violent drug or property crime where the person showed all the good things he or she did since conviction.

In pardon re-applications, the prior application with all the attachments are in the file. You should not resubmit them. Only new information is requested.

This form must also be as complete and truthful as possible (*see* § 12), and it is signed under oath.

Pardon applications are submitted to:

DCC Institutional Release Services (IRS)
Pardon Department
2801 S. Olive St., Suite 6-D
Pine Bluff, AR 71603

Pardon requests also can take up to a year to process.

After a pardon is granted:

You can say that you are not a felon as to the pardoned offense. However, the grant of a pardon will end up in your criminal history and can be seen by those who have a right to see, such as law enforcement and professional licensing boards or agencies.[30]

Any person with a pardoned or discharged sentence may apply to vote.[31]

---

[30] Ark. Code Ann. § 12-12-1007(a)(12).

[31] Ark. Const., Amendment 51, §§ 9(a)(1) ("All persons may register [to vote] who: [¶] (1) Have not been convicted of a felony unless the person's sentence has been discharged or the person has been pardoned; . . . .") & 11(a)(4).

Possession of a firearm is permitted after a pardon [if restoration of gun rights were requested and granted]. Not so with a "time cut," without specific relief from firearms disabilities, and there is a separate place on the form for that.

§ 22. Sealing of pardoned offenses

Under Ark. Code Ann. § 16-90-1411(a)(3), effective January 1, 2014, pardoned offenses are sealed under the the Comprehensive Criminal Record Sealing Act of 2013 (Ark. Code Ann. § 16-90-1401 *et seq.*) except for offenses where the victim is under 18, a sex offense, or an offense resulting in death or physical injury.

§ 23. Relief from firearms disabilities (prohibitions)

One can also seek from the Governor relief from firearms disabilities (prohibitions) so you can go hunting without seeking a pardon.[32] The last page of the Pardon Form, Appendix D, is a form to submit to the local Sheriff to attest that the crime was more than eight years ago and nonviolent. This form is necessary.

State executive clemency alone does not restore the right to possess a firearm under federal law.[33]

§ 24. Death penalty clemencies

In a death penalty case, there is almost always a clemency hearing at least 30 days before a scheduled execution date, unless a clemency request has been waived by the inmate, as some condemned persons in Arkansas have done.

"There are some differences in this process for inmates sentenced to death, as

---

[32] Ark. Code Ann. § 5-73-103 (by implication); *Reynolds v. State,* 18 Ark. App. 193, 197, 712 S.W.2d 329, 331 (1986).
Under federal law, a Governor may restore firearm rights without granting a pardon. 18 U.S.C. § 921(a)(20).

[33] *United States v. Indelicato,* 97 F.3d 627 (1st Cir. 1996); *United States v. Horodner,* 91 F.3d 1317 (9th Cir. 1996).

described in the Supplemental Guidance Pertaining to Death Sentence Cases" in the Policy Manual at p. 21-22, 30:

Supplemental Guidance Pertaining to Death Sentence Cases

In death sentence cases, executive clemency requests must be in the time period described on the application form. When the Governor sets an execution date, the Institutional Release office will cause to be sent to the inmate and the inmate's attorney of record certified letters informing them that an application for executive clemency must be filed no later than 40 days prior to the scheduled execution date. Executive clemency requests filed late will not be considered. The last date on which an application for executive clemency will be accepted will be specified in the letters. This date will be determined by counting back 40 days from the scheduled date of execution, with the day preceding the scheduled date of execution being counted as day 1. If the 40th day is a Saturday, Sunday, or holiday, an application filed on the next business day will be accepted.

At least 30 days prior to the execution date, the Board, with a quorum of members present, must conduct a hearing with the inmate who has submitted an executive clemency request. Additional instructions are at attachment 1. In clemency death sentence cases, a hearing is mandatory.

Attachment 1 provides as follows (also in Appendix A):

1. Any person sentenced to death may apply for executive clemency (Arkansas Constitution, Article 6, Section 18).
2. An application for executive clemency must be filed no later than 40 days prior to the scheduled execution date.
3. An application for executive clemency will be considered as having been duly filed once it is received at the Arkansas Department of Community Correction, Institutional Release Services; 2801 South Olive, Suite 6-D, Pine Bluff, Arkansas 71601.
4. All exhibits or supporting documentation to be considered by the Board of Parole should be attached to the executive clemency application at the time of filing.
5. The application shall set forth the specific reasons or grounds upon

which executive clemency is requested. Failure to set forth specific grounds shall be cause for rejection and return of the application.

6. The Board of Parole, meeting in regular or special session, will interview the inmate concerning his/her request for executive clemency at least 30 days prior to the execution date.

7. The applicant's attorney will submit a list of all persons who will appear at the executive clemency hearing on behalf of the inmate to the Board of Parole and the Warden of the maximum security unit on the day prior to the hearing. The list must show complete names and relationship to the inmate.

8. The time allocated for all presentations and/or testimony by the inmate, attorney and/or witnesses at the executive clemency hearing will be limited to a total of two hours.

9. No more than four (4) persons (the inmate, attorney, and two others) may present arguments and/or testify to the Board of Parole at the executive clemency hearing. The Board will accept written statements by other interested persons.

10. Tape recordings of the executive clemency hearing will not be transcribed, but will be sent directly to the governor with the clemency file and supporting evidence. The inmate is responsible for providing recorders and/or stenographers should a transcript be desired.

11. The Board of Parole's decision will be available within 72 hours after the completion of hearings for the inmate and protesters.

12. The Board Chairperson, with the approval of the Board of Parole, will make an exception to these policies and procedures in the interest of justice.

A "quorum" is at least four members. All seven members vote in death penalty cases. Policy Manual at p. 2.

Ark. Code Ann. § 16-90-506 (Appendix D) applies to death penalty stays of execution, too.

Death penalty clemencies are almost always prepared and presented by a lawyer for the inmate.

Appendices

A   ARKANSAS BOARD OF PAROLE POLICY MANUAL (revised September 26, 2013)

B   Statutes Governing Pardon and Clemency

C   Executive Clemency ("Time Cut") Forms

D   Pardon Forms

Appendix A

Appendix A

ARKANSAS PAROLE BOARD

POLICY MANUAL

(Secretary of State Rule Number 158)

Revised and Adopted September 26, 2013

Table of Contents

Page   **Subject**

1   **Section 1: BOARD MEMBERSHIP, RESPONSIBILITIES, TRAINING, AND OFFICERS**

2   Quorum and General Voting Information
3   Recusal

3   **Section 2: CONSIDERATION OF INMATES ELIGIBLE FOR PAROLE**

3   General Information
3   Risk/Needs Assessments
4   Inmates with Transfer Eligible "TE" Dates
5   Discretionary Transfer (Exceptions to Transfer Eligible "TE" Dates)
5   Inmates with Parole Eligible "PE" Dates
6   Foreign Nationals
6   Time Computation
6   Notification of Officials and Victims
7   Release Hearing Preparation and Guidelines
8   Parole Hearing Panel
8   Transfer Decision Criteria for Release to Parole Status for TE and PE Inmates
8   Conducting a Release Hearing
9   Parole Consideration of Out of State Inmates (Interstate Compact, Act 700)
9   Processing and Transmitting Release Decisions
10   Release Decision Summary
10   Release of an Inmate with an Incurable Illness or who is Permanently Incapacitated (A.C.A. 12-29-204)
10   Modified Release Guidelines for Short-Term Offenders
11   Electronic Monitoring
11   Early Release Program for Offenders to Transitional Housing Facilities
13   Supervision of Parolees
13   Appeal of Board Decision

14   **Section 3: RELEASE REVOCATION**

14   Designee for Conducting Hearings
14   Warrant and Criteria for Arrest of Parolee
14   Waiver of Parole Revocation Hearing
15   New Felony Charges
15   Possible Outcomes of the Revocation Hearing
16   Actions when Revoked
16   Determining the Release Hearing Date
16   Preliminary Hearing Requirement (Interstate Compact Parolees)
17   Release Revocation Process
18   Appeal of Parole Revocation Judge's Revocation Decision

19   **Section 4: EXECUTIVE CLEMENCY**

19   Overview and Terminology
19   Authority for Executive Clemency
20   Eligibility and Application for Executive Clemency
20   Date and Place of Filing

Continued on next page

Page	Subject
20	Required Notice of a Clemency Request and Request for Comment
21	Board Investigation, Review, and Report
21	Hearing Process
22	Supplemental Guidance Pertaining to Death Sentence Cases
22	After the Board Review/Hearing
22	Clemency Appeals
22	**Section 5: BOARD MANAGEMENT AND ADMINISTRATION**
22	Committees of the Board
23	Policy Manual Availability and Review
24	Access to Persons and Records
24	Legal Assistance
24	Inspection of Records
24	Expunging Records (Act 378 Participants)
25	Participation of Parolee in Law Enforcement Undercover Operations
25225	Additional Information about Related Activities Accomplished by Other Agencies
25	Facilities and Equipment
26	Planning, Goals, Objectives, and Program Coordination
26	Financial Processes and Controls
26	Additional Chairperson Duties
26	Personnel and Staffing Guidelines
26	Data Collection, Research, Analysis, and Reports
28	**Section 6: ATTACHMENTS**
29	Form 153 (Law Enforcement Response)
30	Policies and Procedures for Executive Clemency Application by Persons Sentenced to Death
31	Conditions of Release
32	Act 679 Conditions of Release
33	Minimum Length of Stay at Transitional Living Facilities
34	Employee Acknowledgement of Parole Board Policy Manual

Board Approval
September 26, 2013

Signature on File	Signature on File	Signature on File
John Felts	Jimmy Wallace	Richard Mays, Jr.
Chairman	Vice-Chairman	Secretary

Signature on File	Signature on File	Signature on File
Joseph Peacock	Abraham Carpenter, Jr.	Richard Brown, Jr.
Commissioner	Commissioner	Commissioner

Signature on File
Dawne B. Vandiver
Commissioner

Arkansas Parole Board Policy Manual
Revised and Adopted on September 26, 2013

1 - BOARD MEMBERSHIP, RESPONSIBILITIES, TRAINING, AND OFFICERS

The Arkansas Parole Board ("the Board" or "Board") is composed of seven full time members appointed by the Governor and confirmed by the Senate. Each member is appointed for a term of seven years, except that the terms shall be staggered by the Governor so that the term of one member expires each year. If a vacancy should occur on the Board prior to the expiration of a term, the Governor shall fill the vacancy for the remainder of the unexpired term, subject to confirmation by the Senate at its next regular session. The Governor may remove a Board member for good cause as prescribed by law. If the Senate is not in session, confirmation of the removal will be by written petition of a majority of the senators. For those persons eligible for parole, the Board has statutory authority to determine what persons will be placed on parole and to set the time and conditions of the parole. The Board will conduct open meetings and make public its findings for each eligible candidate for parole. However, inmate interviews may be closed to the public at the request of the inmate (Arkansas Code Annotated § 16-93-615).

The Board is also responsible for reviewing all pardon and commutation applications and making non-binding recommendations to the Governor.

Board Members, Parole Revocation Judges, and Support Staff are responsible for carrying out the Board's mission and complying with applicable laws; and all policies within this manual.

Board members must not seek or hold public office which would represent a conflict of interest while on the Board.

Arkansas Code Annotated § 16-93-201 requires that each member must have at least a bachelor's degree from an accredited college or university, and the member should have no less than five (5) years of professional experience in a field listed below. If a member does not have a bachelor's degree from an accredited college or university, they must have (7) years of professional experience in one of the fields listed below:
1. Parole Supervision
2. Probation Supervision
3. Corrections
4. Criminal Justice
5. Law
6. Law Enforcement
7. Psychology
8. Psychiatry
9. Sociology
10. Social Work
11. A related field

The American Correctional Association (ACA) recommends that the racial makeup of the Board should be representative of the diversity of the significant population under its jurisdiction

If the composition of the Board does not meet this standard, the Chairperson will bring this issue to the Governor's attention during the selection process for a new Board member.

Whether or not they have served on the Board previously, a member appointed after July 1, 2011, shall complete a comprehensive training course developed in compliance with guidelines from the National Institute of Corrections, the Association of Paroling Authorities International, or the American Probation and Parole Association.

All members shall complete annual training developed in compliance with guidelines from the National Institute of Corrections, the Association of Paroling Authorities International, or the American Probation and Parole Association.

Training components shall include at a minimum an emphasis on the following subjects:
1. Data-driven decision making
2. Evidence-based practice
3. Stakeholder collaboration
4. Recidivism reduction

All Parole Revocation Judges shall be subject to the same training curriculum developed for members of the Board.

The Governor shall appoint the Chairperson of the Board. The Board shall elect, during the month of February, a Vice Chairperson and a Secretary to serve as officers for the upcoming year. Officers shall be elected by a majority of members present and voting. If an office becomes vacant in the interim, the Board shall elect, at its next regular meeting, a member to serve in that office until the next election. A special election of officers may be called at any time at the request of a majority of the members.

1.1 - Quorum and General Voting Information

A quorum of four members is required to vote on each parole release case. All parole cases reviewed by a single member shall be reviewed by the full Board for agreement prior to a final decision. Such review shall consist of the single member advising the full Board of the following:

1. The inmate's name
2. The inmate's ADC number
3. The inmate's disciplinary class
4. County and year of conviction(s)
5. The inmate's PE/TE and Discharge dates
6. The reason for the member's recommendation(s)

Board practice is to have 7 members vote on executive clemency death sentence cases and a minimum of four votes on other clemency requests.

A member who recuses themselves is not eligible to vote and shall not be counted in determining whether there is a quorum. It is sufficient that a motion, decision, or proposition receives a majority of the votes actually cast. Each Board member has the right to vote on each consideration presented.

Note: No single member may make a request for release to the ADC or DCC without full Board approval in accordance with the rules set forth above.

1.2 - Recusal

No member of the Board or a Parole Revocation Judge should participate in the determination of any matter before them if they:
1. are closely related to the person, the person's attorney, or the victim
2. have had a personal or business relationship with the person, the person's family, the person's attorney, the victim, or the victim's family which would affect or reasonably give the appearance of affecting judgment in the matter
3. have served as counsel for either party in legal proceedings concerning the person
4. have any other interest in the proceeding that would affect or reasonably give the appearance of affecting their judgment in the matter.

The responsibility for determining the appropriateness of recusal under the guidelines established by this policy shall be solely upon that member or Parole Revocation Judge.

In establishing these guidelines for recusal, it is not the intent of the Board to create a right or basis to challenge the actions of this Board, any member of the Board, or Parole Revocation Judge which is not otherwise provided by the laws or Constitution of this State or the United States. In the event a Board member or Parole Revocation Judge abstains or recuses from a vote for parole, transfer, pardon or commutation, this action is final and cannot be changed.

2 - CONSIDERATION OF INMATES ELIGIBLE FOR PAROLE / TRANSFER

2.1 - General Information

"Parole" is the release of an inmate into the community prior to the expiration of the sentence, subject to conditions imposed by the Board and to supervision. Supervision is accomplished on behalf of the Board by Parole/Probation Officers, also referred to as "supervision officers," who work for the Arkansas Department of Community Correction (DCC).

Depending on the date of the offense, some inmates are "transfer eligible," some are "parole eligible," and some inmates are not eligible for parole, but may be considered for release under clemency laws.

The DCC Institutional Release Services (IRS) staff will prepare case records for use by Board members in conducting case reviews and hearings, as required by Arkansas law. Preparation by DCC IRS for an inmate's review shall begin no later than six (6) months prior to that inmate's eligibility date. Board staff will manage these case records to ensure timely review/hearings.

All release hearings will be conducted by a member or members of the Board. However, in situations where there are staffing shortages or high workload, the Chairperson may choose to designate Parole Revocation Judges to conduct release hearings on an interim basis.

2.2 - Risk/Needs Assessments

The Board shall consider the results of a validated risk/needs assessment tool as a part of all release decisions. That same assessment will also influence any conditions of release. The assessment will be administered by staff from ADC and/or DCC in a manner authorized by the

Board.

2.3 - Inmates with Transfer Eligible (TE) Dates

The Arkansas Code Annotated 16-93-614, 615, 616, and 617 allows for the transfer of inmates who have committed certain crimes on or after January 1, 1994, under the provisions of a transfer date, to be transferred to parole status by the ADC subject to rules and regulations promulgated by the Board of Corrections and conditions set by the Board. The electronic Offender Management Information System (eOMIS) assigns a transfer eligibility (TE) date to inmates who are in this "transfer eligible" category (other inmates who are eligible for parole are assigned a "parole eligibility (PE)" date).

When the Board considers an inmate with a TE date the Board will have only two options:

1. Transfer the inmate to the DCC with specified conditions such as supervision level, programming requirements, and facility placement when appropriate. Conditions must be within the current resources of the DCC; or
2. Deny transfer to the inmate, based on established criteria, until the inmate completes a course of action established by the Board that would rectify the Board's concerns. After the completion of the required course of action (which must be within the current resources of the ADC), and final review of the inmate's file to ensure successful completion, the Board will be required to transfer the inmate to the DCC in accordance with administrative policy and subject to conditions attached to the transfer. Should an inmate fail to complete the course of action outlined by the Board to facilitate their transfer to community supervision, it shall be the responsibility of the inmate to petition the Board for a rehearing. In these cases, there will not be an automatic rehearing.

This review may be conducted without a hearing when the inmate has not received a major disciplinary report which resulted in the loss of good time, there has not been a request by a victim to have input on transfer conditions, and there is no indication in the risk/needs assessment review that special conditions need to be placed on the inmate.

A hearing should also be held if an inmate objects to special conditions set by the Board or the Board reverses a previous decision to release the inmate. For cases which only require a review, a Board member may choose to hold a hearing if considered appropriate.

The Institutional Release Officers (IRO) will use eOMIS information and procedural guidance to determine whether the Board can screen an inmate's records and release the inmate without a hearing, or whether a hearing is required. The IRO advises the Board of the options in this regard.

Inmates who are assigned to Varner SuperMax or who are in administrative segregation should be reviewed to determine class and the level of the Varner SuperMax program completion. An inmate may be reviewed by a single member, but the file shall then be forwarded to the full Board for hearing and final determination. Final determination is subject to review by the Board. Unless otherwise determined by a of the Board, an inmate incarcerated at the Varner SuperMax Unit who has failed to attain Level 5 will not be granted a rehearing by the Board unless and until such level has been attained.

2.4 - Discretionary Transfer (Exceptions to Transfer Eligible (TE) Dates)

The following classes of inmates shall be considered for discretionary transfer to the DCC. Discretionary transfer means the Board can deny parole with or without recommending a course of action to the inmate. Even if a course of action is recommended and completed, the Board is not required to release the inmate to community supervision.

- Inmates who, after January 1, 1994, commit Murder in the First Degree, Engaging in a Continuing Criminal Enterprise, or the following Class Y felonies: Kidnapping, Rape, Aggravated Robbery, or Causing a Catastrophe.

- Inmates who on or after July 30, 1999 commit Capital Murder, Murder in the Second Degree, Manslaughter, Negligent Homicide , Sexual Assault in the First Degree, Sexual Assault in the Second Degree, Sexual Abuse in the First Degree, Battery in the First Degree, Domestic Battering in the First Degree, or Simultaneous Possession of Drugs and Firearms.

- Inmates who, on or after February 20, 2013, commit an offense for which they are required upon release to register as a sex offender under the Sex Offender Registration Act of 1997, § 12-12-901 et seq.

- Inmates who, on or after August 16, 2013 commit Attempted Capital Murder, Attempted Murder in the First Degree, any offense listed under A.C.A. § 5-54-201 et seq. (Terrorism-related offenses), or the following Class Y felonies: Attempted Aggravated Robbery, Terroristic Act, Arson, Aggravated Residential Burglary, or Unlawful Discharge of a Firearm from a Vehicle.

The above inmates may be reviewed by a single member but the file shall then be forwarded to the full Board for consideration and then a final determination.

The Board will have the authority to transfer such an inmate at a time when, based on a combination of its members' opinion and a validated risk needs assessment tool, there is a reasonable probability that the inmate can be released without detriment to the community or the inmate.

After the Board has fully considered and denied the transfer of an offender sentenced for committing a discretionary offense, the Board may delay any reconsideration of the transfer for a maximum period of two (2) years.

Note: The same standard of review just listed shall apply to inmates whose crimes were committed prior to January 1, 1994 (Parole Eligible).

2.5 - Inmates with Parole Eligible (PE) Dates

For inmates with a PE date, the Board has discretionary transfer authority. A Board "discretionary transfer" hearing will be conducted for all inmates with a parole eligible (PE) date, unless the inmate waives the hearing in writing. Board members will use the release decision criteria listed on page 8 of this manual as a basis for deciding whether to approve a transfer.

2.6 - Foreign Nationals

Parole consideration must be the same for foreign nationals. Their status or inability to return to their home country must not affect a parole decision. A foreign national may be paroled to their home country when informal arrangements can be made for the transfer and when the inmate consents. The Board shall consider the placement of post-release conditions on offenders released to their home country or an immigration detainer. The condition(s) will take effect upon their reentry to the United States.

2.7 - Time Computation

Within 90 days of incarceration, the ADC will provide inmates who have a TE or PE date with a time card that will provide at a minimum the following information: (1) sentence length, (2) offense, (3) minimum required time to be served before transfer/parole eligibility, (4) jail time credit, (5) class status, and (6) release dates.

2.8 - Notification of Officials and Victims

The Board will use Form 153 (Attachment 1: Law Enforcement Response) to solicit the written or oral recommendations of the sentencing court, the prosecuting attorney, and the sheriff of the county from which the inmate was committed. If the person whose parole is being considered by the Board was convicted of capital murder, of a Class Y, Class A, or Class B felony, or any violent or sexual offense, the Board shall also notify the victim of the crime, or the victim's next of kin, of the parole hearing and shall solicit written or oral recommendations of the victim or their next of kin regarding the granting of the parole. If the prosecuting attorney has notified the Board at the time of commitment of the prisoner that the victim or their next of kin does not want to be notified of future parole hearings, no such notifications will be made. When soliciting recommendations from a victim the Board must notify the victim or his/her next of kin, of the date, time, and place of the parole hearing.

A victim of the crime, or the victim's' next-of-kin, who wish to participate in the victim input process have two responsibilities: (1) notify the Board or its designee of their intention to provide input, and (2) provide current contact information to the Board or its designee.

Supporting documentation from the victim, or the victim's next-of-kin, will be accepted by the Board. In cases involving the transfer of an inmate, the victim, or the victim's next-of-kin, may request and be granted a hearing to provide input concerning the inmate's release conditions only.

At the time that a person is paroled or transferred by the Board, the Department of Community Correction shall give written notice of the granting of the release or transfer to the Sheriff, the Judge, and the Chief(s) of Police of all cities of the first class of the county from which the person was sentenced. If a victim or the victim's next-of-kin has requested notification, notice will also be provided by the Parole/Probation Officer.

If a person is released to a county other than that from which he/she was committed, the Department of Community Correction, or its designee, shall give notice to the Chief of Police or Marshall of all cities to which he/she is released, and the Sheriff of the county to which he/she is released.

A record shall be kept of the actions of the Board. The IRS staff shall notify each institution of decisions relating to persons who are or have been confined therein. The Board will retain a copy of recommendations received and such recommendations will be open to the public during reasonable business hours.

2.9 - Release Hearing Preparation and Guidelines

The Board requires that an inmate receive written notice of parole or transfer hearings at least fourteen days prior to the hearing. An inmate will be notified by the IRO located at their unit through a personal interview. The five objectives of the interview are: (1) to notify the inmate whose hearing is being scheduled to meet the Board, (2) to obtain the inmates signature acknowledging either the "Notice of Hearing" form, a waiver of the hearing, or a deferral of consideration. The original of the form is to be given to the inmate and the pink copy filed in the inmate's State file. A new form is required each time an inmate is scheduled for a hearing, (3) to obtain detailed information regarding the inmate's release plans if parole is granted (4) to provide the inmate with copies of Form 153 statements from sheriffs, judges, and prosecuting attorneys, if any, and (5) to answer any questions the inmate may have regarding parole.

Approximately fourteen days before the hearing the IRS staff will prepare, update and verify a parole file for each inmate being considered for parole or executive clemency. If there is any question as to the accuracy of the information gathered, the staff should verify the accuracy. If the accuracy cannot be verified, the information will be annotated to state this fact. The parole file will contain a voting worksheet for the Board members, a synopsis of the inmate's state file, a Field Report submitted by a Parole/Probation Officer, required legal notices, the results of a validated risk/needs assessment, victim notification information if required, Form 153 responses from sheriffs, judges, and prosecuting attorneys, support and protest correspondence, if any, and prior Boot Camp or parole violation warrants, reports, transcripts, and parole plan. The file is delivered to the Board about one week before interviews at the unit in order for Board members to review prior to the hearing and to refer to the file during the hearing if necessary.

The IRS staff will give the inmate copies of Form 153 responses from sheriffs, judges, and prosecuting attorneys so that the inmate will have information on which the parole decision will be made. If an inmate has requested a victim statement, the request will be forwarded to the DCC Public Relations Office for processing. State law prohibits staff from releasing State criminal justice records to inmates. The IRS staff should advise the inmate that additional confidential information may be considered by the Board such as witness statements and the Board will consider the inmate's work, education, and disciplinary records. When the Board member uses confidential information (that has not been provided to the inmate) as a basis for a decision, the Board member should advise the inmate that confidential information is being used as a basis for the decision.

Each inmate may invite a representative to attend and speak on his/her behalf at the Board hearing. Attorneys will be offered preference to be moved to the top of the docket. There is no limit to the number of visitors an inmate may invite to the hearing. The Board may limit presentations to just one visitor in addition to hearing from the inmate or their representative. There is no age limit. However minors may be barred from the hearing if their presence creates a disruption. Visitors are not required to be on the inmate's Visitation List but must be eligible for it. All visitors must comply with attire and grooming rules. Units will give the utmost consideration to security when admitting visitors to the unit for Board hearings. Victims who arrive at a unit to attend the inmate's hearing will not be admitted to the hearing. Under Arkansas law, the victim is entitled to a separate hearing with the Board.

2.10 - Parole Hearing Panel

The Board may designate a panel for the interviewing of persons for possible parole, transfer and executive clemency. In addition to a Board member or Parole Revocation Judge, a panel may be comprised of one of the following: another Board member, a Parole Revocation Judge, a designated official of the ADC, a designated official of the DCC, or a designated official selected by the Board member interviewing.

2.11 - Transfer Decision Criteria for TE and PE Inmates

Release or discretionary transfer may be granted to an eligible person by the Board when, in its opinion, there is a reasonable probability that the person can be released without detriment to the community or him/herself.

In making its determination regarding a inmate's release or discretionary transfer, the Board must consider the following factors:

1. Institutional adjustment in general, including the nature of any disciplinary actions;
2. When considered necessary, an examination and opinion by a psychiatrist or psychologist can be requested and considered;
3. The record of previous criminal offenses (misdemeanors and felonies), the frequency of such offenses, and the nature thereof;
4. Conduct in any previous release program, such as probation, parole, work release, boot camp or alternative service;
5. Recommendations made by the Judge, Prosecuting Attorney, and Sheriff of the county from which a person was sentenced, or other interested persons;
6. The nature of the release plan, including the type of community surroundings in the area the person plans to live and work;
7. The results of a validated risk/needs assessment
8. The inmate's employment record;
9. The inmate's susceptibility to drugs or alcohol;
10. The inmate's basic good physical and mental health;
11. The inmate's participation in institutional activities, such as, educational programs, rehabilitation programs, work programs, and leisure time activities;
12. The failure of an inmate incarcerated at the Varner Unit Super Max to attain Level 5;
13. When there is a detainer, the Board must pursue the basis of any such detainer and only release the inmate to a detainer where appropriate. A detainer must not be considered an automatic reason for denying parole.

2.12 - Conducting a Release Hearing

All hearings will be conducted in privacy, and all individual case information will be kept confidential. Prior to the hearing, Board members must review information available in writing about the offender's prior history, current situation, events in the case since any previous hearing, information about the offender's future plans and relevant conditions in the community. The Board member conducting the hearing is responsible for making a record of the major issues and findings in the hearing report.

The Chairman, in consultation with Board staff and staff from the ADC and DCC, will decide if video conferencing will be used at a given hearing and who will participate by way of video conferencing. Video conferencing is an appropriate option in certain circumstances, including the following; to meet urgent deadlines, when severe weather conditions prevent the safe travel of Board members, or when it would be the most effective and efficient use of manpower and budgetary resources.

In advance of the hearing, the inmate will be notified about their hearing may be conducted via video. If it is apparent that participating in a hearing conducted via video will create an undo hardship due to a documented disability, the Chairman will make arrangements for certain accommodations and/or ensure that an inmate is seen in person.

2.13 - Parole Consideration of Out-Of-State Inmates (Interstate Compact, Act 700)

The Board will transfer or consider for parole those eligible persons serving sentences outside the State in the following manner:

When an inmate confined in the prison system of another state or the federal system becomes eligible for transfer or parole in Arkansas, as indicated by a certified copy of a Judgment and Commitment Order from a court of this state, the appropriate records office of the ADC shall notify the DCC IRS office.

Before taking action on a transfer or parole request by an out-of-state inmate, the DCC IRS office will request, in writing, that the corresponding board or commission in the jurisdiction where the person is incarcerated, provide the following information: 1) For all cases, a validated risk assessment evaluation; 2) For cases with a PE date, a recommendation and supporting documentation as to whether the person should be released.

The Board will use the information provided in lieu of the person's personal appearance before the Board. The Board will also consider information about the person and his/her crime provided by parole staff, law enforcement agencies, the victim(s) (or the victim(s)' next-of-kin), public officials, the person being considered, and other interested persons.

All other provisions of Arkansas law pertaining to transfer and/or the granting or denying of parole to persons held by the state shall apply.

2.14 - Processing and Transmitting Release Decisions

The Department of Community Correction IRS office is the designated entity for processing all Board decisions relating to parole/transfer (grant, denial, or deferral) and Executive Clemency (a recommendation of with or without merit). The Board will record all votes in eOMIS and transmit both an electronic and paper copy to IRS. The record of the votes in eOMIS will then be audited by DCC IRS staff to ensure correctness. Once all votes have been verified, the IRS staff will forward a record of votes to each Institutional Release Officer (IRO) at the various ADC and DCC units.

Prior to releasing a vote to an inmate, the IRO will once again verify that all information regarding the inmate's parole is correct. The decision of the Board will then be given to the inmate in a manner consistent with unit policy. Refer to the "Release Decision Summary" section below for additional information.

It is the responsibility of the IRO to contact the appropriate unit staff if an inmate is required to complete any program(s) prior to release. The IRO is also responsible for any other action requested regarding the Board's decision.

The specific date of an inmate's release will be set by the inmate's unit of assignment. The IRO is the designated party for conveying that date to the inmate.

2.15 - Release Decision Summary.

A person considered by the Board for release will be advised in writing of the Board's decision within 21 days from the date of the hearing. The notification will include the Board's action and the most significant reason(s) for that action. The needs for safety and security within each unit prescribe that no information concerning the vote on the possible release of an inmate will be made until such date determined by the Board following the ratification of voting held at a regularly scheduled meeting of the Board.

Vote sheets are used in every decision making process done by the Board and are available upon request from the DCC Public Information Office.

2.16 - Release of an Inmate with an Incurable Illness or who is Permanently Incapacitated (Arkansas Code Ann. §12-29-404)

When, in the independent opinions of a prison physician and a consultant physician from Arkansas, an inmate has an incurable illness which, on the average, will result in death within twenty-four (24) months, or when an inmate is permanently incapacitated, the Director of the ADC or the Director of the DCC shall make these facts known to the Board.

The Board shall request all such information that is germane to making a decision. If the facts warrant and the inmate's physical condition no longer makes them a threat to public safety, the Board may approve the inmate for immediate transfer to parole supervision.

An inmate is not eligible for parole under this section if:
1. They are required to registered as a sex offender under Arkansas Code Ann. §12-12-901 et seq. and
2. The inmate is assessed as a Level Three (3) or higher; or
3. A victim of one or more of the inmate's sex offenses was 14 years of age of younger

The Board may revoke an inmate's parole supervision granted under this section if, after notification, it is determined that the offender's medical condition improves to the point that they would initially not have been eligible under these guidelines.

2.17 - Modified Release Guidelines for Short-Term Offenders

Arkansas Code Annotated § 16-93-710, authorizes the Board to set modified hearing guidelines for offenders who have a sentence of 2 years or less and become Transfer Eligible while in the county jail.

Upon notification of an offender's eligibility by the ADC, the DCC shall immediately make all necessary notifications to law enforcement officials and victims (See "Notification of Officials and Victims"), schedule the offender for a hearing, and assemble the hearing file for the Board's review. The ADC shall expedite the intake of eligible offenders.

The Board shall consider the file as a screening. All other standard hearing processes shall be followed.

At the discretion of the Board, eligible offenders may be paroled directly from the County Jail Back-up List. If an offender is to be released directly from the County Jail Back-up List, their file must be reviewed by the Board no later than 6 months prior to their eligibility date. The Board shall work collectively with both ADC and DCC to develop guidelines for these offenders.

- Any offender convicted under A.C.A. § 5-4-501(c)(2) or of a Class Y felony shall be ineligible for release under this option. As determined by the county sheriff, an offender who has committed a violent or sexual act while incarcerated in a county jail facility shall be ineligible for release under this option.

For offenders with a sentence greater than two years, the Board shall establish procedures sufficient to mitigate the risk of those offenders becoming Transfer Eligible while in the county jail. The Board Chairman shall designate an employee of the Board to regularly review the ADC County Jail Back-up List and compile the names of offenders whose intake needs to be expedited by the ADC. This compiled list shall consist of those individuals who are within 6 months of becoming Transfer Eligible but may be expanded in scope as the need arises. This list shall contain at a minimum the names, ADC #, and county where these offenders are being held. Once this list is certified by the Board Chairman or their designee, it shall be transmitted to the ADC and they shall in turn schedule these offenders for intake.

Once these individuals are brought in to the Department, ADC shall notify DCC-Institutional Release Services of their Intake. DCC shall immediately begin the process of scheduling these offenders for the next upcoming Board. Offenders with non-discretionary convictions and those without an active conviction for a sexual offense shall be transmitted to the Board as a screening. Offenders whose conviction is discretionary and those who have an active conviction for a sexual offense shall be scheduled for a hearing. Offenders convicted of "Failure to Register" on a discharged registerable offense shall be scheduled for a screening.

2.18 - Electronic Monitoring of Offenders

Based on the pre-established criteria in Arkansas Code Ann. §16-93-711, the Director of ADC or DCC will request the Board consider the release of certain inmates to electronic monitoring after they have served 120 days of their sentence. The Board will consider these offenders under the normal guidelines that apply to the screening process.

Inmates released under this section shall remain on electronic monitoring for at least 90 days or until their transfer eligibility date, whichever is sooner.

2.19 - Early Release Program for Offenders to Transitional Housing Facilities
Act 679 of 2005

Offenders held in the Department of Correction (ADC), other than those excluded below, shall be eligible for early release to a transitional housing facility, or an equivalent entity, licensed by the Department of Community Correction (DCC) up to one (1) year prior to the offender's date of eligibility for parole or transfer. An offender's home or the residence of an offender's family member shall not be considered a transitional housing facility for the purposes of this program.

Offenders released under this program must reside at an approved transitional housing facility until they reach their eligibility date.

It is determined that there is a reasonable probability that an offender within one (1) or more or the following categories cannot be placed in a transitional housing facility under the provisions of this program without posing a detriment to the community or the offender. Therefore an offender is not eligible for this program if:

1. They have failed to maintain Class I or II status at the time of petition or between the time of their hearing and release to the transitional housing facility.
2. They have served less than 6 months in the Department of Correction. Time served in the county jail shall not be counted toward program eligibility.
3. They have been convicted of any of the following:
    a. Any homicide, §§ 5-10-101 – 5-10-105
    b. Battery in the first degree, § 5-13-201
    c. Domestic battering in the first degree, § 5-26-303
    d. Kidnapping, § 5-11-102
    e. Aggravated robbery, § 5-12-103
    f. Causing a catastrophe, § 5-38-202(a)
    g. Engaging in a continuing criminal enterprise, § 5-64-405
    h. Simultaneous possession of drugs and firearms, § 5-74-106
4. They have been convicted of any offense requiring registration under § 12-12-903 (Sex Offender Registration Act of 1997).
5. They have been convicted of any offense determined by the Board to, by its nature or definition, involves violence, the threat of violence, the potential threat of violence, or the disregard for the safety of the lives of others.
6. They have received a disciplinary or conviction (§§ 5-54-110 – 5-54-112) for behavior related to an escape, or an attempted escape, from the ADC, DCC, or a law enforcement agency.

Eligible offenders shall submit a written petition the Board for consideration under this program through their unit Institutional Release Officer. Once a petition has been received and the offender's eligibility has been determined, the offender shall be scheduled for an Act 679 hearing before the Board. Hearings scheduled under this program shall follow the distribution of all applicable notices under § 16-93-615 and all applicable policies established by the Board pertaining to a parole/transfer hearing (to include the right to appeal a denial of eligibility or release) and by the Department of Community Correction (DCC) pertaining to parole plan approval.

Inmates released under this program shall be supervised by officers of the DCC under the guidelines of the Act 679 Conditions of Release established by the Board (see Board Manual Attachments). The conditions must be based on a reasoned, rational plan developed in conjunction with validated risk-needs assessment and include at minimum a curfew requiring an offender placed in a transitional housing facility under this program to present themselves at a scheduled time to be confined in the transitional housing facility.

An offender who without permission leaves the custody of the transitional housing facility in which he or she is placed may be subject to criminal prosecution for escape,

§§ 5-54-110 – 5-54-112. Facilities receiving an offender released under this program shall be provided with information by DCC on reporting an offender who without permission leaves the custody of the facility prior to their eligibility date.

Revocation of placement in transitional housing must follow the revocation proceedings established in § 16-93-705.

2.20 - Supervision of Parolees

Supervision of parolees is done on behalf of the Board, by the Department of Community Correction. In consultation with the Board, DCC is authorized to establish written policies and procedures for the supervision of parolees. The supervision of parolees shall be based on evidenced-based practices including a validated risk/needs assessment. Decisions shall target the parolee's criminal risk factors with appropriate supervision and treatment designed to reduce the likelihood to reoffend. Further guidance for parole supervision can be found in Arkansas Code Ann. §16-93-712

Every parolee, while on release, shall be subject to the orders of the Board. Failure to abide by any of the conditions as instructed may result in revocation of his/her conditional release.

Every inmate receives a written copy of his/her supervision conditions from the Parole/Probation Officer and signs that they understand their release conditions. A Parole/Probation Officer may request that a supervision condition be amended or removed entirely. All requests for the amending or removal of a condition must be made in writing to the Board. Any request for exemption of a special condition must be approved by the Board.

At any time during a parolee's conditional release, the Board may issue a warrant for the arrest of the parolee for violation of any conditions of release or may issue a notice to appear to answer a charge of a violation. The Board will not issue a notice to appear without an accompanying warrant. The warrant and notice shall be served personally upon the parolee. The warrant shall authorize all officers named therein to place the parolee in custody at any suitable detention facility pending a hearing.

Any Department of Community Correction officer may arrest a parolee without a warrant or may deputize any officer with power of arrest to do so by giving the officer a written statement (or white warrant) setting forth that the parolee, in the judgment of the Department of Community Correction officer, violated conditions of the parolee's release. The written statement (or white warrant) delivered with the parolee by the arresting officer to the official in charge of the detention facility to which the parolee is brought shall be sufficient warrant for detaining the parolee pending disposition.

2.21 - Appeal of Board Decision

An inmate or his/her attorney may request reconsideration of any parole decision of the Board within sixty days of the release of the vote. Written requests for reconsideration shall be submitted to the Board. Only one reconsideration request will generally be considered by the Board for a particular Board action.

3 - RELEASE REVOCATION

3.1 - Designee for Conducting Hearings

The Board's designee for conducting release revocation hearings is the Parole Revocation Judge.

3.2 - Warrant and Criteria for Arrest of Parolee

When a parolee has committed a violation (other than those referenced in the following paragraph) that results in a violation report, a warrant is issued when the parolee's presence in the community, pending disposition of a Revocation Hearing, would present unreasonable risks to public or individual safety or when it is very likely that the parolee will abscond. Supervision officers shall utilize violation reports to provide the information necessary for the Board to determine if these criteria have been met. The Board will review violation reports and issue warrants only when the criteria are met. However, the evidence does not need to rise to the same standard of probable cause required for arrest and criminal charges. This does not prohibit the supervision officer from arresting the parolee with a "white warrant" for detaining the parolee while waiting for a Board warrant.

If a parolee has been charged with a felony involving violence, as defined under § 5-4-501(d)(2) or a felony requiring registration under the Sex Offender Registration Act of 1997, § 12-12-901 et seq., the Board shall issue a warrant for the arrest of the parolee. Supervision officers shall utilize the violation report to provide the information necessary to issue a warrant under this paragraph. The violation report must be received by the Board within 7 calendar days after the supervision officer becomes aware of the charges; unless a waiver has been granted by the Board or its designee.

A parolee arrested on a warrant issued under the previous paragraph shall be detained pending a mandatory Revocation Hearing.

3.3 - Waiver of Parole Revocation Hearing

When an offender has committed a serious technical violation or repeated pattern of minor violations, and the parolee meets eligibility requirements established by written policy of the DCC for the Technical Violator Program (TVP), the Board authorizes a supervision officer to prepare a violation report, give notice to the parolee and transport the parolee to the TVP if provided the parolee knowingly and intelligently signs a hearing waiver.

An offender may knowingly and intelligently waive his/her right to a hearing and be returned to the ADC. A waiver to the ADC must be signed by a member of the Board or a Parole Revocation Judge. An offender returned to the ADC on a hearing waiver shall be eligible for release consideration after a minimum of six (6) months.

An offender shall be made aware of his/her right to knowingly and intelligently waive his/her right to a hearing prior to the hearing. At this point the offender shall also be made aware of the possible outcomes of a Revocation hearing.

If a hearing waiver is granted, the parolee may subsequently appeal the waiver to the Board. An appeal of a hearing waiver shall be made in the manner listed below. However the filing of an appeal may not suspend the transport of an offender to the ADC or TVP.

- The appeal must be made in writing by the parolee or his/her attorney to the Board within thirty (30) days from the date the hearing waiver is signed by the parolee unless the time period or other requirements are waived by the Board.

- In the written appeal, the parolee or his/her attorney may request a general review of the hearing waiver only and ask that it be rescinded and a hearing be scheduled. The parolee or his/her attorney should state in the appeal specific reasons for the belief that the hearing waiver should be reversed.

- The appeal shall be presented to the Board as soon as practical after it is received. The Board may request statements in response to the appeal from a Parole Revocation Judge and/or the parolee's supervising officer.

3.4 - New Felony Charges

When a new felony is committed and the parolee is not held on a Board-issued warrant, the Parole Revocation Judge may choose to hold or postpone the Revocation Hearing. If the Revocation Hearing is postponed, the Parole Revocation Judge can choose to conduct a hearing later, such as when new violations occur. If postponed and the court sentences the parolee to time at the ADC, the Board processes an administrative revocation (no hearing).

When a parolee receives a new felony conviction and is sentenced to prison, his/her release may be revoked without a hearing. Written notice of this action will be forwarded to the parolee with a copy to the state file. If the parolee's conviction is set aside on appeal or otherwise nullified, his/her release will be reinstated, unless the Board or its designee has previously found there to be a preponderance of the evidence, after a hearing, that the parolee inexcusably violated one or more conditions of release. This finding justifies revocation notwithstanding the lack of a conviction for a criminal offense.

3.5 - Possible Outcomes of the Revocation Hearing

If a parolee is found to have violated a condition(s) of their release, the Parole Revocation Judge may still return the parolee to supervision, impose additional conditions of release or revoke his/her release and specify whether the violator should be sent to the TVP (when eligible) or the ADC.

The Parole Revocation Judge should consider the range of alternatives for sanctions and/or treatment. The following alternatives are generally actions that are considered and/or used by the supervision officer for minor violations, before resorting to a violation report. However, the following alternatives may be used in lieu of revocation: increased supervision level, referral to a counseling program or service, referral to a resource agency or program appropriate to the offense, the loss of meritorious good time accrual status (good time earned while in parole status to reduce the time required to be under active supervision), a letter of reprimand, verbal warning, electronic monitoring, or curfews. The Parole Revocation Judge may confer with the supervision officer to determine the best course of action. An offender should only be returned to prison after considering less severe sanctions and treatment programs, and when it is determined to be in the clear interest of the public.

3.6 - Actions When Revoked

If then offender's supervision is revoked, the Parole Revocation Judge will complete appropriate sections of the "ADC Disposition of Revocation Hearing" form for Boot Camp program parolees or the "Arkansas Parole Board Disposition of Parole Revocation Hearing" forms for all other parolees. The Parole Revocation Judge will enter the month when the parolee is to be scheduled to appear before the Board using the criteria in the following section. This month is entered even when the parolee is sent to the TVP because the parolee may subsequently be transferred to ADC for disciplinary reasons in which case the date would apply.

3.7 - Determining the Release Hearing Date

On the disposition of revocation hearing form, the Parole Revocation Judge will indicate the month the parolee will be scheduled for a release hearing. The Parole Revocation Judge may revoke an offender's release for up to one year.

3.8 - Preliminary Hearing Requirement (Interstate Compact Parolee)

When the sending state has issued a warrant, a preliminary hearing must be held within 14 days from the time the warrant was served with one exception. The exception is made if the parolee has admitted to one or more significant violations of supervision conditions.

The Parole Revocation Judge must forward any evidence or record generated during a probable cause hearing through the DCC Interstate Compact Office to the sending state.

When a preliminary hearing for an Interstate Compact Parolee is required, Parole Revocation Judges usually schedule and conduct a revocation hearing within the allowable 14-day time period, thereby making it unnecessary to conduct a preliminary hearing. When a parolee is incarcerated and there is a white warrant and/or Board-issued warrant, a preliminary hearing must be held within 14 days from the date the warrant was served unless one of the following conditions applies:

1. The parolee voluntarily, knowingly and intelligently waives his/her right to a hearing after being informed of rights pertaining to the hearing and the consequences of waiving the hearing, or
2. The violation report is substantiated by a court conviction or a court finding of probable cause on new criminal charges, or
3. A revocation hearing was held, or
4. The Parole Revocation Judge has determined there is good cause for delay or postponement of the hearing and this is documented; for example, the parolee or his/her attorney may request postponement of the hearing.

A preliminary hearing follows the same procedures as a revocation hearing with the following exceptions:

1. The result of the preliminary hearing is not a finding of guilt, but a finding that there is probable cause to hold a revocation hearing. A finding of probable cause justifies a longer period of incarceration pending a revocation hearing.
2. Extenuating and mitigating factors do not need to be considered at a preliminary hearing because the finding is one of probable cause. Extenuating and mitigating factors can instead be discovered in a revocation hearing.

3.9 - Release Revocation Process

At a revocation hearing, the Parole Revocation Judge must seek and consider evidence that supports or counters the violation charges as well as any extenuating or mitigating circumstances that suggest that the violation does or does not warrant revocation of the parolee's supervision.

Parole Revocation Judges must allow the parolee and their attorney, when present, to exercise the right to:

1. Present evidence and favorable witnesses;
2. Seek disclosure of evidence;
3. Confront adverse witness(es), unless the witness(es) would be subjected thereby to a risk of harm;
4. Have counsel of choice present or, in the case of indigent parolees who request assistance to adequately present their case, have counsel appointed; however, the Parole Revocation Judge may determine that the situation does not justify the expense of a lawyer; and
5. Request postponement of the hearing for good cause.

The Supervising Officer will:

1. Request a warrant when an arrest is considered necessary;
2. Arrest and jail a parolee only when criteria are met;
3. Advise parolee of hearing related rights to include the rights Parole Revocation Judges must allow as described in the previous paragraph ;
4. Give the parolee notice of the violation;
5. Offer the parolee an opportunity to sign a hearing waiver when TVP-eligible;
6. Give scheduled parolees 72 or more hours notice of scheduled hearing;
7. Transport jailed parolees to scheduled hearings;
8. Be present at hearings to provide supplemental information and security;
9. Use criteria to set the release hearing month for parolees sent to the TVP (this date is for a release hearing if the revoked parolee is subsequently transferred from the TVP to ADC);
10. Transport parolees to the TVP or arrange transportation to ADC as appropriate; and
11. Process any additional supervision conditions.

The Parole/Probation Area Manager (or designee) will notify the Board of parolees who require a hearing by providing a prioritized list so that the Board may schedule hearings.

To ensure compliance with ACA standards, the Board will hold hearings within 14 days for detained parolees and within 60 days for parolees who are not detained.

The Parole Revocation Judge will:

1. Hold a preliminary revocation hearing as described above when required. A revocation hearing may be held in lieu of a preliminary hearing with the exception of Interstate Compact cases.

2. Hold a revocation hearing within 60 days from the date of the violation report when a preliminary hearing has been held or is not required, unless the parolee has signed a hearing waiver (or requested a postponement of the hearing).
3. Conduct a hearing where the parolee resides or near the community where the violation is alleged to have occurred or where the parolee has been taken into custody; the Parole Revocation Judge may be at a remote location using a telephone or video conference system.
4. Complete the hearing results and give 3 signed copies of the hearing report to the supervising officer. This hearing report will include a statement of the reasons for the determination made and the evidence relied upon to include a summary of documents presented and responses made at the preliminary / regular hearing.

The Supervising Officer will:

1. Provide one copy of the hearing report to the parolee after appropriate restraints are in place (if the decision is to not revoke the parolee, restraints would not be necessary since the parolee would be released to community supervision). If not received the day of the hearing, a parolee who has been revoked will receive their copy within 21 calendar days of the hearing.
2. Keep one copy for their records;
3. Provide the other copy to the receiving facility (TVP or ADC).

3.10 - Appeal of Parole Revocation Judge's Revocation Decision

A parole violator may appeal the Parole Revocation Judge's decision by submitting a written appeal to the Board. Filing of an appeal will not preclude sending the release violator to the TVP or ADC. However, a Parole Revocation Judge may choose to suspend sending the violator to the TVP or ADC when the Parole Revocation Judge is aware of an appeal or intent to appeal, and if the violator has not yet been taken to the TVP or ADC.

An appeal of release revocation or the placement of additional conditions is made in the following manner:

1. The appeal must be made in writing by the parolee or his/her attorney to the Board within thirty (30) days from the date of the revocation hearing disposition unless the time period or other requirements are waived by the Board.

2. In the written appeal, the parolee or his/her attorney may request a general review of the decision to revoke and ask that the decision be reversed. The parolee or his/her attorney should state in the appeal specific reasons for the belief that the decision should be reversed.

3. The appeal shall be presented to the Board as soon as practicable after it is received. The report of the designee containing a summary of the evidence presented at the revocation hearing, the decision of the designee, and the reasons for the decisions shall also be presented to the Board.

Upon the consideration of the appeal, the Board shall vote:

1. to affirm the decision of the Parole Revocation Judge;
2. to reverse the decision of the Parole Revocation Judge's, or
3. to schedule an appearance by the parolee before the Board for further consideration.

If the parolee is scheduled to appear before the Board, he/she will be afforded the same rights he/she was afforded at the revocation hearing.

4 - EXECUTIVE CLEMENCY

4.1 - Overview and Terminology

Clemency means kindness, mercy, forgiveness and leniency. Executive Clemency is sometimes referred to in this section as "clemency."

Executive Clemency is the process through which the Governor considers requests for granting reprieves, commutations of sentence and pardons after conviction and considers requests to remit (forgive) fines and forfeitures.

A reprieve is a temporary relief from or postponement of execution or criminal punishment or sentence. A reprieve is merely a stay (delay) of the execution of the sentence for a certain time period which is typically given to allow an offender an opportunity to reach an agreement on a change to the imposed sentence.

A respite is a temporary suspension of the execution of a sentence.

Commutation means a permanent change of sentence or punishment such as changing a death sentence to a life sentence without parole. Commutations are usually requested by incarcerated persons. Incarcerated persons submit requests through the IRO.

A pardon request asks that a criminal record be removed from the public record. A pardon is usually requested by a person who is no longer incarcerated. Persons who are not incarcerated submit applications directly to the DCC IRS office in Pine Bluff where background information is gathered.

All requests are then forwarded to the Board for investigation. After the investigation, the Board provides a report and recommendation to the Governor. Important guidance about the executive clemency process can be found in the following sections, in attachment 1, on the application form, and in supplemental guidance published in a governor's memo.

4.2 - Authority for Executive Clemency

The Arkansas Constitution, Article 6, Section 18, gives the Governor pardoning power as follows:

"In all criminal and penal cases, except in those of treason and impeachment, the Governor shall have power to grant reprieves, commutations of sentence and pardons after conviction; and to remit fines and forfeitures under such rules and regulations as shall be prescribed by law. In cases of treason he shall have power, by and with the advice and consent of the Senate, to grant reprieves and pardons; and he may, in the recess of the Senate, respite the sentence until the adjournment of the next regular session of the General Assembly. He shall communicate to the General Assembly at every regular session each case of reprieve, commutation or pardon, with his reasons therefore, stating the name and crime of the convict, the sentence, its date and the date of the commutation, pardon or reprieve."

4.3 - Eligibility and Application for Executive Clemency

The eligibility criteria for the various forms of executive clemency are listed on the applications. A person who is incarcerated may request an application form from IRO unless the applicant has a pending clemency request. The incarcerated person must return the completed application to the IRO. Once an application is submitted for screening and/or consideration, the process cannot be interrupted.

For persons who are not currently incarcerated, an application form can be obtained from, and completed applications sent to, the Arkansas Department of Community Correction, Institutional Release Services; 2801 South Olive, Suite 6-D, Pine Bluff, Arkansas 71601.

Applications for commutations and pardons may also be obtained from the Board's office during normal business hours or from their website. Applications obtained from the Board must still be sent to DCC IRS for processing.

Inmates serving a death penalty must file an application for executive clemency as described in the application form. Further information on the application process can be found on pages 19 of this manual.

An application for executive clemency must set forth the grounds upon which the pardon or commutation is sought. Following are examples of grounds upon which an application may be filed: (1) to correct an injustice which may have occurred during the person's trial; (2) life threatening medical condition (also see Ark. Code Ann. §12-29-404) (3) to reduce an excessive sentence; or (4) the person's institutional adjustment has been exemplary, and the ends of justice have been achieved.

Any person who files for clemency and is denied by the Governor shall not be eligible to reapply for a period of four (4) years from the date of application. If the applicant is serving a life sentence without parole for a crime other than Capital Murder, they will not be eligible to reapply for six (6) years from the date of denial. If an applicant is serving a sentence of life without parole for a conviction of Capital Murder, they will not be eligible to reapply for eight (8) years from the date of denial. However, a person who is denied by the Governor, can petition the Board for a waiver of the waiting period.

4.4 - Date and Place of Filing

An application for executive clemency will be considered as having been filed when it is received by DCC IRS. The address is on the application form.

4.5 - Required Notice of a Clemency Request and Request for Comment

In addition to any other requirements, the Executive Clemency Coordinator will solicit the written or oral recommendations from the sentencing court the prosecuting attorney, and the sheriff of the county from which the person was committed.

If the inmate is serving a sentence for capital murder (Ark. Code Ann. §5-10-101 and 5-4-607(a)(1)) or a Class Y, Class A, or Class B felony, copies of the application will be filed with the Secretary of State, the Attorney General, the Sheriff of the county in which the offense was committed, the Prosecuting Attorney of the judicial district in which the applicant was found guilty and sentenced and the Circuit Judge who presided over the proceedings at which the applicant was found guilty and sentenced or his/her successor.

If the inmate is serving a sentence for capital murder (Ark. Code Ann. §5-10-101), the application will also be published by the Executive Clemency Coordinator by placing two insertions, separated by a minimum of seven (7) days, in a newspaper of general circulation in the county in which the applicant committed the offense.

For crimes described in this section, the Executive Clemency Coordinator will send notification of the person's application to the victim(s) (or the victim(s)' next-of-kin), at their last known address(es), when the victim/next-of-kin has registered to receive such notices. The notice will solicit a written or oral recommendation.

The Executive Clemency Coordinator will use eOMIS to ask the Parole/Probation Officer to prepare a field report. As part of a field report, the officer contacts the prosecuting attorney and asks whether there are any victims or next-of-kin who have requested notification (and checks eOMIS for this information). If there are, the officer sends them notification of the clemency application and informs the Executive Clemency Coordinator of this action. When the suspense date for comments has passed, the Executive Clemency Coordinator assembles a file and sends it to the Board for consideration.

4.6 - Board Investigation, Review, and Report

At least four Board members will individually review each clemency file. Board members will vote to recommend that clemency be granted, denied, or to schedule the person for a hearing before the Board (a hearing is required for death sentence cases, see above details). If any Board member requests a hearing, a hearing will be scheduled. Board members may request supplemental information or take other reasonable actions to ensure a complete investigation prior to making a decision. The file is then returned to the DCC IRS, Executive Clemency Coordinator.

If a hearing is granted, the Executive Clemency Coordinator will notify the victim(s) of the crime, or the victim's' next-of-kin, and will ask the IRO to schedule a hearing at least 30 days from the time notice of the hearing was given to the victims(s) of the crime, or the victim's' next-of-kin.

4.7 - Hearing Process

An applicant for executive clemency who appears before the Board may be accompanied by supporters, including his/her attorney. If the person is not incarcerated in this state, his/her appearance before the Board is not necessary. The Board shall consider the statements of the applicant and a spokesperson, the applicant's file, reports from law enforcement, a pre-sentence report and any documentary evidence presented by the applicant or other interested persons, including the victims(s) of the crime, or the victim's' next-of-kin. On the basis of this information, the Board will vote (1) to recommend that clemency be granted, or (2) to recommend that clemency be denied. If the Board recommends that clemency be granted, it may specify the nature and terms of the commutation being recommended. There are some differences in this process for inmates sentenced to death, as described in the "Supplemental Guidance Pertaining to Death Sentence Cases" paragraph.

4.8 - Supplemental Guidance Pertaining to Death Sentence Cases

In death sentence cases, executive clemency requests must be in the time period described on the application form. When the Governor sets an execution date, the Institutional Release office will cause to be sent to the inmate and the inmate's attorney of record certified letters informing them that an application for executive clemency must be filed no later than 40 days prior to the scheduled execution date. Executive clemency requests filed late will not be considered. The last date on which an application for executive clemency will be accepted will be specified in the letters. This date will be determined by counting back 40 days from the scheduled date of execution, with the day preceding the scheduled date of execution being counted as day 1. If the 40th day is a Saturday, Sunday, or holiday, an application filed on the next business day will be accepted.

At least 30 days prior to the execution date, the Board, with a quorum of members present, must conduct a hearing with the inmate who has submitted an executive clemency request. Additional instructions are at attachment 1. In clemency death sentence cases, a hearing is mandatory.

4.9 - After the Board Review/Hearing

The Board shall submit to the Governor its recommendation, a report of the investigation, and all other information the Board may have regarding the applicant (Ark Code Ann. §16-93-204). All applications for executive clemency considered by the Board, with the non-binding recommendation will be forwarded to the Governor for final action.

4.10 - Clemency Appeals

There is no appeal of the Board's recommendation. There is no appeal of the Governor's decision. When the situation merits a new clemency application may be submitted, subject to the statutory timeframes listed on page 20 of this manual.

5 - BOARD MANAGEMENT AND ADMINISTRATION

5.1 - Committees of the Board

In order to further its oversight of agency operations, the Board shall establish certain committees comprised of members of the Board which shall monitor operational areas and/or address certain issues. Members of the Board's support staff may be invited to provide information at the request of a committee. However, only members of the Board shall have the ability to vote in a committee meeting.

Committees of the Board shall be designated as either "Standing" or "Special." The formation, scope, and membership of Standing Committees are established by the provisions of this Manual and may only be altered following the policy revision process outlined in the "Policy Manual Availability and Review" section of this Manual. The Board Chair may refer issues to a Standing Committee not specially listed in its mission and/or scope but which are related to its subject matter. Appointments to Standing Committees shall occur during the same February meeting as the election of Vice-Chair and Secretary. Special Committees may be established at the discretion of the Board Chairman or upon request of four (4) members of the Board. The scope, duration, and membership of Special Committees shall be limited by the discretion of the Board Chair or by (4) members of the Board.

The following are Standing Committees of the Board:

Fiscal Committee – This committee is responsible for monitoring the fiscal activities of the Board and ensuring that appropriate fiscal controls are in place. It is also responsible for making policy recommendations to the Full Board regarding budget, procurement, inventory control, and other related functions. Three (3) working days prior to a Full Board Meeting, the Fiscal Support Supervisor, or another designated employee, shall file with the Board Chair and Fiscal Committee Chair a report detailing the previous month's expenditures. That same report shall be presented at the upcoming Full Board Meeting. The report shall contain expenditures by General Ledger Code and provide the remaining fund balance(s) at the end of the reporting period. Membership of the Fiscal Committee shall consist of no less than (3) three Board members but no more than four (4) Board members appointed by the Board Chair. One of the members must be the Board's Vice-Chair who shall Chair the Fiscal Committee.

Personnel Committee – This committee is responsible for establishing and recommending changes to agency personnel policies to include but not limited to changes in the Board's Employee Manual and applicable Administrative Directives. The Personnel Committee Chair is responsible to for coordinating an annual review of the Employee Manual and reporting the findings of that review to the Full Board. In consultation with the Board Chair, this committee is responsible for reviewing applicants for vacant positions within the agency and making hiring/promotion recommendations to the Full Board. At least one (1) member of this committee shall sit on all applicant interview panels. Membership of the Personnel Committee shall consist of no less than (3) three Board members but no more than four (4) Board members appointed by the Board Chair. One of the members must be the Board's Secretary who shall Chair the Personnel Committee.

The Fiscal Committee is required to meet at least monthly and be prepared to report during Full Board meetings or upon request. All other committees shall meet at the call of the Committee Chair, Board Chair, or upon the referral of an issue from the Full Board. Committee Chairs are required to provide adequate notice to the Administrative Services Manager of their committee's meeting schedule to allow for the required public notification. Committee Chairs are also responsible for filing a written summary of their meetings with the Administrative Services Manager. No committee action shall be considered final until it has been ratified by the Full Board. The only exceptions to this requirement are instances where the Full Board gives advance consent for a committee to take final action on an issue.

The Board Chair shall serve as an ex-officio member on all committees.

5.2 - Policy Manual Availability and Review

The Board Chairperson will ask the ADC and DCC to make this policy manual readily available to inmates, residents and parolees. The Board Chairperson will also ensure the policy is available to staff and the public. The Board Chairperson will initiate an annual review by all Board members of the Board's policies and will ensure that revisions and updates are undertaken when necessary. The Board's designee for maintaining this policy manual is the Administrative Services Manager.

Revisions to this policy manual must receive a favorable vote by a majority of the Board. Revisions shall not take immediate affect until they have been through the promulgation process outlined in the Administrative Procedure's Act unless an emergency has been declared by a majority of the Board.

5.3 - Access to Persons and Records

All ADC and DCC officials have a legal duty to grant to Board members and properly accredited Board representatives, access at all reasonable times to any person over whom the Board has jurisdiction, to provide facilities for communicating with and observing such persons, to furnish the Board such reports as the Board shall require concerning the conduct and character of any person in the custody of the ADC or DCC, and to provide any information deemed pertinent by the Board in determining whether a person shall be released.

5.4 - Legal Assistance

Board members may seek legal advice from the DCC Staff Attorney or an assigned attorney at the State Attorney General's Office. The State Attorney General will represent the Board when required.

5.5 - Inspection of Records

The Board staff will not release information to inmates or the public unless authorized in this manual or in writing by the Board Chairperson. All requests for information should be forwarded to the Department of Community Correction Public Information Office.

Parole and Executive Clemency Files – Pursuant to the provisions of Ark. Code Ann. §16-93-202, the following portions of Parole and Clemency files will be provided by the DCC Public Relations Office for inspection upon request by a person having a proper interest therein and whenever the interests or welfare of the person involved make inspection desirable or helpful: 153 forms, Executive Clemency (commutation & pardon) applications, and vote worksheets. The Public Relations Office may release other information unless restricted by law. The Board Chairperson or Public Relations Office may release information to researchers and others involved in monitoring or studying the criminal justice system unless restricted by law.

5.6 - Expunging Records (Act 378 Participants)

A person sentenced to the Department of Correction under Act 378 of 1975, as amended (Ark Code Ann. §16-93-501 *et seq.*), shall receive an expungement of his/her records by the following process:

After the person discharges the entire sentence imposed by the Court, a report will be submitted by the ADC to the Board Chairperson. After reviewing the information, the Chairperson shall approve an expungement, if required by law.

Upon approval, the Chairperson, or their designee, shall complete a Certificate of Expungement, which shall be forwarded to the person by the ADC staff.

The ADC staff will notify all pertinent law enforcement agencies and the Circuit Clerk's office(s) that the person's record has been expunged. The record will then be sealed and sequestered, to be made available only to law enforcement or judicial officials.

5.7 - Participation of Parolee in Law Enforcement Undercover Operations

The Board will not authorize a parolee to participate in any Law Enforcement Undercover Operation. However, the DCC Director may authorize parolee participation in undercover investigations in a manner consistent with DCC policy.

5.8 - Additional Information about Related Activities Accomplished by Other Agencies

In addition to related tasks described elsewhere in this manual, other agencies accomplish the following tasks in support of the Board's mission.

The agency to which an offender is committed (ADC or DCC) will promptly inform every registered victim and next-of-kin of the offender's estimated date of release from incarceration, as well as each of the following events:
- An escape from a correctional facility or community program;
- A recapture;
- A decision of the Governor to commute the sentence or to pardon;
- A release from incarceration and any conditions attached to the release; and
- The offender's death

5.9 - Facilities and Equipment

The Chairperson will ensure staff has adequate equipment and space with appropriate privacy as necessary for the effective and efficient processing of business.

5.10 - Planning, Goals, Objectives, and Program Coordination

The Chairperson must accomplish the following:

1. Participate in Board of Corrections meetings to facilitate planning.
2. Meet at least annually with the ADC and DCC Directors, and as necessary with the Sentencing Commission to coordinate programs and facilitate joint State-wide planning.
3. Meet at least semiannually with the director(s) of institutions from which parole is granted.
4. Ensure the Board has written long-range goals and related objectives and that these are reviewed, updated as needed, and evaluated for progress.
5. Maintain regular liaison with appropriate legislative committees, during at least each regular session of the legislature, for the purposes of offering advice and opinions on appropriate legislative matters.

The Chairperson or designee will meet at least annually with the administrative staff of the parole investigation and supervision agency to ensure a means exists for coordinating efforts, to undertake joint planning, and to agree on means of implementing and evaluating such plans. The Chairperson a or designee will meet at least annually with representatives of relevant criminal justice agencies, police, prosecution and courts to develop a means of coordinating programs, to undertake joint planning and to agree on means of implementing and evaluating such plans.

Each Board member will visit one or more institutions and a representative sample of community facilities at least annually, specifically for the purpose of meeting with staff and inmates/residents to exchange information about programs, institutional operations, and parole policies and procedures. The Chairperson, as the chief administrative officer of the Board, is exempted from this requirement. Minutes or notes from such visits must be provided to the Accreditation Coordinator.

Board members and –s Parole Revocation Judges must initiate ongoing interaction with the Parole/Probation Services staff through such means as conferences, seminars, training sessions, and visits to field offices.

5.11 - Financial Processes and Controls

The Board must have a budget system which links continuing basis agency functions and activities to the costs necessary for their support. There must be a clearly defined budget which provides for personnel, operating, and travel costs sufficient for the operation of the Board. The Chairperson must ensure the budgetary process includes financial controls and monitoring of expenses. The Chairperson must ensure a detailed budget request is submitted and must participate in the legislative budget allocation process. In preparing the budget, input from Board members and staff must be solicited.

5.12 - Additional Chairperson Duties

The Chairperson has the following additional administrative responsibilities:

1. Coordinate Board member work schedules and job assignments
2. Chair Board meetings
3. Serve as the official spokesperson, however, he/she may use the DCC Public Information Officer as a media spokesperson as long as the Chairperson ensures that the Public Information Officer fully understands the Board policies and positions on matters of public interest.
4. Organizing, controlling, and tracking the work of the Board's staff.

5.13 - Personnel & Staffing Guidelines

The Chairperson will from time to time assess the staffing mix to determine it reasonably matches the local population in terms of racial mix, thereby meeting or exceeding the intent of the affirmative action program. When necessary, deficiencies will be documented and an affirmative action plan will be put in place. Pay rates will also be assessed to ensure they compare favorably with comparable positions in the community.

Parole Revocation Judges must have a minimum of a Juris Doctorate unless there is documented justification of experience that can be reasonably substituted. At least 2/3 of the Parole Revocation Judges must have at 3 or more years experience in a criminal justice or juvenile justice experience, or equivalent experience in a relevant profession

5.14 - Data Collection, Research, Analysis, and Reports

The Board will gather data throughout the year from such sources as eOMIS. At least annually the Board will review and analyze the parole decision-making, statistical, and research data.

Consistent with confidentiality requirements, the Chairperson or his/her designee will collaborate with criminal justice and human service agencies on programs of information gathering, exchange, and standardization, including national data collection efforts.

Board and staff members and external research professionals are encouraged to conduct research.

Board members and designated staff will work with researchers in deciding which questions should be addressed, which data should be gathered, and how data should be presented.

The Board Chairperson must review and approve all research study plans before implementation. This review should ensure the privacy interests of offenders and other parties for the cases under study are protected.

The Board Chairperson and others involved in parole decision-making will use statistical and research data among other factors in making decisions and policy development.

The Board and staff will use the eOMIS as a key element in their research and decision-making system.

The Board will collect data for outcome measures by using eOMIS or other means. Outcome measures may be based on ACA recommendations, the uniform parole reporting system, or internally developed data elements. As part of this process, the Chairperson or designated staff members will obtain information from eOMIS at least quarterly.

Custom reports, to display eOMIS data suitable for outcome measures and special studies, may be requested from the DCC Research and Evaluation section.

The Chairperson will ensure results of significant research projects are provided to the appropriate staff and others. Additionally, copies will be made available to the public upon request.

Beginning October 1, 2011, the Board shall file, in an electronic format, a monthly report to the Chairs of the House and Senate Judiciary Committees, the Legislative Council, the Board of Corrections, the Governor's Office, and the Commission on Disparity in Sentencing. This report shall contain the number of persons who make application for parole and those who are granted or denied parole during the previous month for each criminal offense classification, a breakdown by race of all persons sentenced in each criminal offense classification, the reason for each denial of parole, the results of the risk-needs assessment, and the course of action that accompanies each denial pursuant to § 16-93-615(a)(2)(B)(ii).

The Board will also file an annual report with the Governor's Office and the General Assembly before February 1 of each year for the preceding year. The report shall be filed in an electronic format with the General Assembly and shall be submitted only to the Speaker of the House, the President Pro Tempore of the Senate, the lead sponsor of the legislation authorizing preparation of the report, and the Director of the Bureau of Legislative Research. The report shall contain statistical and other data concerning the work of the Board, including research studies which it may make on parole or related functions. A copy of the report shall be published to the Board's website.

The Board shall cooperate with, and upon request make presentations and provide various reports, to the extent the Board's budget will allow, to the Legislature. The presentations shall consist of a review of Board policy and discretionary offender programs and services.

6 - ATTACHMENTS

Attachment 1	Form 153 – Law Enforcement Response
Attachment 2	Policies and Procedures for Executive Clemency Application by Persons Sentenced to Death
Attachment 3	Conditions of Release
Attachment 4	Act 679 Conditions of Release
Attachment 5	Minimum Length of Stay at Transitional Living Facilities
Attachment 6	Employee Acknowledgement of Board Policy Manual

FOR EXAMPLE PURPSOES ONLY. AN OFFICIAL FORM WILL BE GENERATED BY DCC INSTITUTIONAL RELEASE SERVICES.

Arkansas Parole Board
Transfer Eligibility (TE) Applicants
Legal Notice – Form 153 (Law Enforcement Response)

Date:_____   Time:_____

To: _____

_____

_____

Re: _____ ADC #: _____ Location: _____

TE Date _____ Board Hearing Date: _____

The Parole Board requests your recommendation on the above-named inmate who is scheduled to be interviewed for Transfer Eligibility.

Our file(s) contain the following information:

County	Docket	Crime	Counts	Sentence Date
Total Sentence Length: _____		Minimum Release Date _____		

This individual is scheduled to appear before the Board for consideration of Transfer Eligibility in the near future. The Board is requesting your comments which will be placed in his file and considered when reviewing for Transfer Eligibility. If the Board defers action for one year, an additional recommendation will be requested. **List specific reasons for your support or opposition to this individual's transfer. Attach additional pages if necessary.**

Response: _____

_____

_____

_____

_____

Return form to: DCC Institutional Release Services 2801 South Olive St, Suite 6-D Pine Bluff, AR 71601	Signed: _____ Title: _____ Date: _____

ARKANSAS PAROLE BOARD
POLICIES AND PROCEDURES FOR EXECUTIVE CLEMENCY APPLICATION
BY PERSONS SENTENCED TO DEATH

1. Any person sentenced to death may apply for executive clemency (Arkansas Constitution, Article 6, Section 18).

2. An application for executive clemency must be filed no later than 40 days prior to the scheduled execution date.

3. An application for executive clemency will be considered as having been duly filed once it is received at the Arkansas Department of Community Correction, Institutional Release Services; 2801 South Olive, Suite 6-D, Pine Bluff, Arkansas 71601.

4. All exhibits or supporting documentation to be considered by the Board should be attached to the executive clemency application at the time of filing.

5. The application shall set forth the specific reasons or grounds upon which executive clemency is requested. Failure to set forth specific grounds shall be cause for rejection and return of the application.

6. The Board, meeting in regular or special session, will interview the inmate concerning their request for executive clemency at least 30 days prior to the execution date.

7. The applicant's attorney will submit a list of all persons who will appear at the executive clemency hearing on behalf of the inmate to the Board and the Warden of the maximum security unit on the day prior to the hearing. The list must show complete names and relationship to the inmate.

8. The time allocated for all presentations and/or testimony by the inmate, attorney and/or witnesses at the executive clemency hearing will be limited to a total of two hours.

9. No more than four (4) persons (the inmate, attorney, and two others) may present arguments and/or testify to the Board at the executive clemency hearing. The Board will accept written statements by other interested persons.

10. Tape recordings of the executive clemency hearing will not be transcribed, but will be sent directly to the governor with the clemency file and supporting evidence. The inmate is responsible for providing recorders and/or stenographers should a transcript be desired.

11. The Board's decision will be available within 72 hours after the completion of hearings for the inmate and protesters.

12. The Board Chairperson, with the approval of the Board, will make an exception to these policies and procedures in the interest of justice.

Signature on File	**January 28, 2010**
Parole Board Chairperson	**Date**

Arkansas Parole Board
Conditions of Release

1. **REPORTS.** You must report to your supervising officer the next day after you are released unless that day is a weekend or holiday. In such cases you must report the next day the Parole Office is open. Thereafter, you must report as instructed by your supervising officer. All written and oral statements made by you to your supervising officer must be truthful.

2. **EMPLOYMENT/EDUCATION.** You must maintain approved employment or be enrolled in an approved education program unless otherwise directed. You must obtain permission from your supervising officer before quitting your employment or education program. If you lose your job or are terminated from your education program, you must notify your supervising officer within 48 hours.

3. **RESIDENCE AND TRAVEL.** You must obtain prior approval from you supervising officer to change your place of residence, stay away from your approved residence overnight, or leave your assigned county.

4. **LAWS.** You must obey all federal and state laws, local ordinances and court orders. You are required to pay all court-ordered fines, fees, and/or restitution. You must report any citations or summons to your supervising officer on the next regular workday. You must report in person following your release from an arrest, release from parole hold, and any other contact with law enforcement authorities on the next regular workday.

5. **WEAPONS.** You must not own, possess, use, pawn, sell or have under you control any firearm (or imitation) or other dangerous weapon, or be in the company of any person possessing such weapons. You must not possess any ammunition.

6. **ALCOHOL/CONTROLLED SUBSTANCES.** You will avoid the excessive use of alcohol, or abstain completely if directed, and will stay out of bars, taverns, clubs, and liquor stores. You must not sell, deliver or possess, or use controlled substances except as prescribed by a physician. You will submit yourself to random testing for the use of intoxicants and/or controlled substances.

7. **ASSOCIATION.** You must not associate with convicted felons, persons who are engaged in criminal activity, or other persons with whom your supervising officer instructs you not to associate. (Association with convicted felons at work, in counseling programs, in church, or in other locations and circumstances specifically approved by the Parole Board or your supervising officer is not prohibited).

8. **SUPERVISION FEES.** You must pay a monthly supervision fee unless granted an exemption. Community service work in lieu of supervision fees may be required.

9. **COOPERATION.** You must, at all times, cooperate with your supervising officer and the Parole Board. You must submit yourself to any rehabilitative, medical, or counseling program that the Parole Board or your supervising officer deems appropriate.

10. **SEARCH AND SEIZURE.** You must submit your person, place of residence, and motor vehicles to search and seizure at any time, day or night, with or without a search warrant, by any Department of Community Correction officer.

11. **WAIVER OF EXTRADITION.** Your acceptance of conditional release constitutes an agreement to waive extradition to the State of Arkansas from any jurisdiction in or outside the United States where you may be found, and you also agree that you will not contest any effort by any jurisdiction to return you to the State of Arkansas to answer a charge of violation of any of the conditions of your release.

12. **SPECIAL CONDITIONS.** The Board may set special conditions and the parolee must abide by any special conditions set by the Board, e.g., mental health, alcohol and/or drug abuse treatment program, or community service in lieu of fee exemption.

Arkansas Parole Board
Act 679 Conditions of Release
(For Offenders Released under Act 679 of 2005)

1. **EMPLOYMENT:** You must maintain approved employment to be housed in the Transitional Living Facility. You must obtain permission from the Transitional Living Facility staff before quitting your employment. Termination from employment will result in removal from the Transitional Living Facility.

2. **RESIDENCE:** You must be physically located at the Transitional Living Facility at all times unless you are at an approved employment site.

3. **LAWS:** You must obey all federal and state laws, local ordinances and court orders. You are required to pay all court ordered fines, fees and restitution. You must report any arrest, citation, or summons to your supervising officer within 48 hours.

4. **WEAPONS:** You must not own, possess, use, pawn, sell, or have under your control any firearm (or imitation) or other dangerous weapon, or be in the company of any person possessing such weapons. You must not possess any ammunition.

5. **ALCOHOL/CONTROLLED SUBSTANCES:** You will avoid the use of alcohol and all controlled substances. You must not sell, deliver, possess, or use controlled substances except as prescribed by a physician. You will submit yourself to random testing.

6. **COOPERATION:** You must, at all times, cooperate with the Transitional Living Facility staff, Arkansas Parole Board, Arkansas Department of Community Correction Staff, and Arkansas Department of Corrections Staff.

7. **SEARCH & SEIZURE:** You must submit your person and/or property to search and seizure at any time, with or without, a search warrant, whenever requested to do so by Department of Community Correction Staff, or Transitional Living Facility Staff.

8. **SPECIAL CONDITIONS:** I agree to abide by the specific rules and conditions promulgated by the Transitional Living Facility to which I am being released. A signed copy of these rules will be attached to this document.

A Resolution of the Arkansas Parole Board
Regarding Minimum Length of Stay at Transitional Living Facilities
Approved and Adopted on June 14, 2012

WHEREAS, the mission of the Arkansas Parole Board ("the Board" or "Board") is to "promote public safety by the return of offenders into the community through supervised conditional release."

WHEREAS, page 8 of the Arkansas Parole Board Manual (as of May 17, 2012) requires among other things that the Board considers (1) "The nature of the release plan, including the type of community surroundings in the area the person plans to live and work. (2) The results of a validated risk/needs assessment. (3) The offender's susceptibility to drugs or alcohol and (4) The offender's basic good physical and mental health."

WHEREAS, the Board allows offenders to parole out to a licensed Transitional Living Facility.

WHEREAS, Transitional Living Facilities generally provide treatment programs and support services to their residents.

WHEREAS, the Board realizes the value of these treatment programs and support services in the reintegration of offenders in to the community.

WHEREAS, a period of 90 days has been determined, through communication with parole supervision staff and management of Transitional Living Facilities, to be an adequate time period to deliver these treatment programs and support services.

WHEREAS, Arkansas law establishes that every offender, while under parole supervision, shall be subject to the orders of the Board.

NOW THEREFORE BE IT RESOLVED, that the Arkansas Parole Board during its June 14, 2012 Board meeting passed this Resolution in establishment of a mandatory standard requiring offenders to remain at the Transitional Living Facility they are initially released to for a period of no less than 90 days. This requirement shall remain in effect until a written waiver has been received from the Board.

Signature on File	Not in Attendance at Meeting	Signature on File
John Felts Chairman	Jimmy Wallace Vice-Chairman	Richard Mays, Jr. Secretary

Not in Attendance at Meeting	Signature on File	Signature on File
Carolyn Robinson Commissioner	Abraham Carpenter, Jr. Commissioner	Joseph Peacock Commissioner

Signature on File		
Richard Brown, Jr. Commissioner		

Employee Acknowledgement of Parole Board Policy Manual

Please acknowledge by signing that you have read and understood the Arkansas Parole Board Policy Manual.

All employees or officials of the Arkansas Parole Board are responsible for complying with all pertinent policies. The Fiscal/Human Resources Section will place a signed copy of this form in your personnel file.

This form must be signed and returned within five days of receipt.

Employee Acknowledgement:

_____	_____
PRINT NAME	**SIGNATURE**
_____	_____
SECTION	**DATE**

Supervisor's Confirmation:

_____	_____
PRINT NAME	**SIGNATURE**
_____	_____
SECTION	**DATE**

Appendix B

Appendix B

STATUTES GOVERNING PARDON AND CLEMENCY

§ 16-93-207 **Applications for pardon, commutation of sentence, remission of fines and forfeitures.**

§ 5-4-607 **Capital murder, Class Y, A, B felonies; Application for executive clemency — Regulations.**

§ 16-90-1411 **Sealing of records for a pardoned person – Pardons for youthful felony offenders.**

§ 16-90-506 **Death penalty cases. Reprieve, new trial, etc.**

Ark. Code Ann. § 16-93-207, Applications for pardon, commutation of sentence, and remission of fines and forfeitures.

(a)(1)   (A) At least thirty (30) days before granting an application for pardon, commutation of sentence, or remission of fine or forfeiture, the Governor shall file with the Secretary of State a notice of his or her intention to grant the application.

(B) The Governor shall also direct the Department of Correction to send notice of his or her intention to the judge, the prosecuting attorney, and the sheriff of the county in which the applicant was convicted and, if applicable, to the victim or the victim's next of kin.

(2) The filing of the notice shall not preclude the Governor from later denying the application, but any pardon, commutation of sentence, or remission of fine or forfeiture granted without filing the notice shall be null and void.

(b) If the Governor does not grant an application for pardon, commutation of sentence, or remission of fine or forfeiture within two hundred forty (240) days of the Governor's receipt of the recommendation of the Parole Board regarding the application, the application shall be deemed denied by the Governor, and any pardon, commutation of sentence, or remission of fine or forfeiture granted after the two-hundred-forty-day period shall be null and void.

(c)(1)   (A) Except as provided in subdivision (c)(3) and subsection (d) of this section, if an application for pardon, commutation of sentence, or remission of fine or forfeiture is denied in writing by the Governor, the person filing the application shall not be eligible to file a new application for pardon, commutation of sentence, or remission of fine or forfeiture related to the same offense for a period of four (4) years from the date of filing the application that was denied.

(B) Any person who made an application for pardon, commutation of sentence, or remission of fine or forfeiture that was denied on or after July 1, 2004, shall be eligible to file a new application four (4) years after the date of filing the application that was denied.

App. B, p. 3

(2) If an application for pardon, commutation of sentence, or remission of fine or forfeiture is denied by the Governor pursuant to subsection (b) of this section, the person filing the application may immediately file a new application for pardon, commutation of sentence, or remission of fine or forfeiture related to the same offense.

(3)   (A) The Parole Board may waive the waiting period for filing a new application for pardon, commutation of sentence, or remission of fine or forfeiture described in subdivision (c)(1)(A) of this section if:

(i) It has been at least twelve (12) months after the date of filing the application that was denied; and

(ii) The Parole Board determines that the person whose application was denied has established that:

(a) New material evidence relating to the person's guilt or punishment has been discovered;

(b) The person's physical or mental health has substantially deteriorated; or

(c) Other meritorious circumstances justify a waiver of the waiting period.

(B)(i) The Parole Board shall promulgate rules that shall establish policies and procedures for waiver of the waiting period.

(ii) The Parole Board may make additions, amendments, changes, or alterations to the rules in accordance with the Arkansas Administrative Procedure Act, § 25-15-201 et seq.

(d)(1) Except as provided in subdivision (d)(3) of this section, if an application for pardon, commutation of sentence, or remission of fine or forfeiture of a person sentenced to life imprisonment without parole is denied in writing by the Governor, the person filing the application shall not be eligible to file a new application for pardon, commutation of sentence, or remission of fine or forfeiture related to the same offense for a period of:

(A) Six (6) years from the date of the denial; or

(B) Eight (8) years from the date of the denial if the applicant is serving a sentence of life without parole for capital murder,

§ 5-10-101.

(2) If an application for pardon, commutation of sentence, or remission of fine or forfeiture of a person sentenced to life imprisonment without parole is denied by the Governor pursuant to subsection (b) of this section, the person filing the application may immediately file a new application for pardon, commutation of sentence, or remission of fine or forfeiture related to the same offense.

(3)(A) The Parole Board or the Governor may waive the waiting period for filing a new application for pardon, commutation of sentence, or remission of fine or forfeiture described in subdivision (d)(1) of this section if:

(i) It has been at least twelve (12) months after the date of filing the application that was denied; and

(ii) The Parole Board determines that the person whose application was denied has established that:

(a) New material evidence relating to the person's guilt or punishment has been discovered;

(b) The person's physical or mental health has substantially deteriorated; or

(c) Other meritorious circumstances justify a waiver of the waiting period.

(B)   (i) The Parole Board shall promulgate rules that shall establish policies and procedures for waiver of the waiting period.

(ii) The Parole Board may make additions, amendments, changes, or alterations to the rules in accordance with the Arkansas Administrative Procedure Act, § 25-15-201 et seq.

(e) If an application for pardon, commutation of sentence, or remission of fine is granted, the Governor shall:

(1) Include in his or her written order the reasons for granting the application; and

(2) File with the Senate and the House of Representatives a copy of the order that includes:

(A) The applicant's name;

(B) The offense of which the applicant was convicted;

(C) The sentence imposed upon the applicant;

(D) The date that the sentence was imposed; and

(E) The effective date of the pardon, commutation of sentence, or remission of fine.

(f)   (1) This section shall not apply to reprieves.

(2) Reprieves may be granted as presently provided by law.

HISTORY: Acts 1993, No. 5, §§ 1-4; 1995, No. 1195, § 1; 1999, No. 498, § 2; 2005, No. 1975, §§ 4, 5; 2005, No. 2097, § 2; 2007, No. 183, § 1; 2011, No. 1169, § 1; 2013, No. 131, §§ 1, 2.]

Ark. Code Ann. § 5-4-607: Capital murder, Class Y, A, B felonies; Application for executive clemency — Regulations.

(a)   The pardon of a person convicted of capital murder, § 5-10-101, or of a Class Y felony, Class A felony, or Class B felony, or the commutation of a sentence of a person convicted of capital murder, § 5-10-101, or of a Class Y felony, Class A felony, or Class B felony, may be granted only in the manner provided in this section.

(b)(1)   A copy of the application for pardon or commutation shall be filed with:

(A)   The Secretary of State;

(B)   The Attorney General;

(C)   The sheriff of the county where the offense was committed;

(D)   The prosecuting attorney of the judicial district where the applicant was found guilty and sentenced, if still in office, and, if not, the successor of that prosecuting attorney;

(E)   The circuit judge presiding over the proceedings at which the applicant was found guilty and sentenced, if still in office, and, if not, the successor of that circuit judge; and

(F)   The victim of the crime or the victim's next of kin, if he or she files a request for notice with the prosecuting attorney.

(2)(A) The application shall set forth a ground upon which the pardon or commutation is sought.

(B) If the application involves a conviction for capital murder, § 5-10-101, a notice of the application shall be published by two (2) insertions, separated by a minimum of seven (7) days, in a newspaper of general circulation in the county or counties where the offense or offenses of the applicant were committed.

(c) On granting an application for pardon or commutation, the Governor shall:

(1) Include in his or her written order the reason for the granting of the application; and

(2) File with the House of Representatives and the Senate a copy of his or her written order which shall state the:

(A) Applicant's name;

(B) Offense of which the applicant was convicted and the sentence imposed;

(C) Date of the judgment imposing the sentence; and

(D) Effective date of the pardon or commutation.

(d) A person sentenced to death or to life imprisonment without parole is not eligible for parole and shall not be paroled.[1]

(e) If the sentence of a person sentenced to death or life imprisonment without parole is commuted by the Governor to a term of years, the person shall not be paroled, nor shall the length of his or her incarceration be reduced in any way to less than the full term of years specified in the order of commutation or in any subsequent order of commutation.

(f) A reprieve may be granted as presently provided by law.

[Note: Footnote added.]

---

[1] To the same effect is Ark. Code Ann. § 5-4-606. Life in Arkansas is life.

HISTORY: Acts 1975, No. 280, § 1306; 1977, No. 474, § 13; A.S.A. 1947, § 41-1306; Acts 1991, No. 706, § 1; 1993, No. 741, § 1; 1999, No. 498, § 1; 2001, No. 201, § 1; 2003, No. 1169, § 1; 2005, No. 1975, § 1; 2005, No. 2097, § 1.]

§ 16-90-1411. Sealing of records for a pardoned person -- Pardons for youthful felony offenders. [Effective January 1, 2014.]

(a)   (1) The Governor shall notify the court upon issuing a pardon, and the court shall issue an order sealing the record of a conviction of the person pardoned.

(2) The record of a conviction relating to the conviction of a person pardoned before July 15, 1991, shall be sealed upon the filing of a copy of the pardon with the court by the person.

(3) This section does not apply to a pardon issued for:

(A) Any offense in which the victim is a person under eighteen (18) years of age;

(B) A sex offense; or

(C) An offense resulting in death or serious physical injury.

(b) A person shall have his or her record of a conviction sealed by the court if the person:

(1) Committed a felony in this state while under sixteen (16) years of age;

(2) Was convicted and given a suspended sentence;

(3) Received a pardon for the conviction; and

(4) Has not been convicted of another criminal offense.

(c) This section does not prevent a person from requesting that his or her criminal record be sealed under § 16-90-1405 or § 16-90-1406.

[HISTORY: Acts 2013, No. 1460, § 9.]

Ark. Code Ann. § 16-90-506. Death penalty cases. Reprieve, new trial, etc.

(a)(1)   Should the condemned felon, while in the custody of the Director of the Department of Correction, be granted a reprieve by the Governor or obtain a writ of error from the Supreme Court or should the execution of the sentence be stayed by any competent judicial proceeding, notice of the reprieve or writ of error or stay of execution shall be served upon the Director of the Department of Correction, as well as upon the condemned felon, and he or she shall yield obedience to it.

(2)   In any subsequent proceeding, the mandate of the court having regard to the condemned felon shall be served upon the Director of the Department of Correction as well as upon the felon.

(3)   If the felon is resentenced by the court, the proceedings shall be as provided under the original sentence.

(b)   If a new trial is granted to the condemned felon after he or she has been conveyed to the Department of Correction, he or she shall be conveyed back to the place of trial as the Director of the Department of Correction may direct.

(c)   The only officers who shall have the power of suspending the execution of a judgment of death are:

(1)   The Governor;

(2)   In cases of insanity or pregnancy of the individual, the Director of the Department of Correction as provided in subsection (d) of this section; and

(3)   In cases of appeals, the Clerk of the Supreme Court, as prescribed by law.

(d)(1)(A)   When the Director of the Department of Correction is satisfied that there are reasonable grounds for believing that an individual under sentence of death is not competent, due to mental illness, to understand the nature and reasons for that punishment, the Director of the Department of Correction shall notify the Deputy Director of the Division of Behavioral Health of the Department of Health and Human Services. The Director of the Department of Correction shall also notify the Governor of this action. The Division of Behavioral Health of the Department of Health and Human Services shall cause an inquiry to be made into the mental condition of the individual within thirty (30) days of receipt of notification. The attorney of record of the individual shall also be notified of this action, and reasonable allowance will be made for an independent mental health evaluation to be made. A copy of the report of the evaluation by the Division of Behavioral Health of the Department of Health and Human Services shall be furnished to the Department of Correction Mental Health Services, along with any recommendations for treatment of the individual. All responsibility for implementation of treatment remains with the Department of Correction Mental Health Services.

(B)(i) If the individual is found competent to understand the nature of and reason for the punishment, the Governor shall be so notified and shall order the execution to be carried out according to law.

(ii) If the individual is found incompetent due to mental illness, the Governor shall order that appropriate mental health treatment be provided. The Director of the Department of Correction may order a reevaluation of the competency of the individual as circumstances may warrant.

(2) When the Director of the Department of Correction is satisfied that there are reasonable grounds for believing that a female convict under sentence of death is pregnant, he or she shall suspend the execution until it appears that she is not pregnant or until she has delivered the child.

[HISTORY: Crim. Code, §§ 290, 291; Acts 1913, No. 55, §§ 6, 7; C. & M. Dig., §§ 3250, 3251, 3258, 3259; Pope's Dig., §§ 4095, 4096, 4103, 4104; Acts 1959, No. 228, §§ 1, 2; A.S.A. 1947, §§ 43-2617, 43-2618, 43-2621, 43-2622; Acts 1993, No. 914, § 1.]

Appendix C

State of Arkansas
Commutation (Time-Cut) Application

Instructions

A Commutation (time cut) is not a right but a discretionary duty of the Governor that can be denied for any reason. An applicant for Commutation (time cut) should understand that the process will take several months, even a year or more in some instances.

The Parole Board must review all applications. After the Parole Board makes the review and recommendation, you will be notified. Please, do not call the Parole Board concerning results.

The Governor relies on the recommendation of the Parole Board and will not review any application, which has not been first reviewed by the Parole Board. **The Governor does not review files taken out of order.** There is no appeal process for Commutation (time cuts). If the Governor denies the application, that decision is final.

Incorrect information will be grounds for denial.

You must answer all questions or your application will be returned.

Attach additional pages if necessary to answer questions.

Type or print this application using blue or black ink pen.

If not incarcerated send application to:
DCC Institutional Release Services (IRS)
Executive Clemency Department
2801 S. Olive St. Suite 6-D
Pine Bluff, AR. 71603

**IF INCARCERATED SEND APPLICATION THROUGH
Institutional Release Officer (IRO) at your unit of assignment**

Commutation (time cut) Application

Institutional Release Services
2801 S. Olive St. Suite 6-D
Pine Bluff, AR. 71603
870-543-1027 / 870-879-6725 (fax)

Name _____   Date of Birth_____

Address_____   Race _____Sex_____

City_____   ADC# _____

State _____Zip_____   SS#_____

Home Phone #_____   Cell phone #_____

∎∎

Person preparing the application if other than yourself:

Name: _____

Address _____

Telephone numbers (home): _____ (work): _____

Is the person preparing the application an attorney? Yes ___ No ___ AR bar # _____

Reason for Requesting a Commutation (time cut)

1. ____ **I wish to correct an injustice which may have occurred during the trial. I have attached letters or other documentation that will support this claim. (If you wish to attach explanations or statements to this application, it will be considered as a part of the application.)**

2. ____ **I have a life-threatening medical condition which does not qualify for Act 290. I have attached a statement explaining my condition. (You must provide a medical information release in order for the Board to view your medical records.)**

3. ____ **I want to adjust what may be considered an excessive sentence.**

4. ____ **My institutional adjustment has been exemplary and the ends of justice have been achieved.**

All supporting documentation must be available when the Board considers your application.

App. C, p. 2

1. You must list below, **ALL CRIMES WHICH YOU WANT COMMUTED (time cut)**.

Crime	County of conviction	Date	Court Docket number	Sentence	Date of discharge

2. Were there victims in your crimes? YES _____ NO _____ If so, how many? _____
   If yes, answer the following questions:

   Did you know the victim? YES _____ NO _____

   a. If yes, what was the relationship? _____

   b. Was the victim injured? _____

   c. Age of the victim _____

   d. Was the victim a law enforcement or public official? _____

3. Were other persons involved in the crimes listed above? Yes _____ No _____
   if yes, list the names of your accomplices and what, if any, sentences they received.

Name	Sentence

App. C, p. 3

4. Concerning the facts of the crimes, **briefly** explain what happened in each case. _____

_____

_____

_____

_____

_____

_____

_____

5. Explain why you think the Governor should grant you a commutation (time cut). _____

_____

_____

_____

_____

_____

6. Describe what you have done to demonstrate your rehabilitation. (Community programs, volunteer work, furthering education, speaking engagements, mentoring to others, etc.) ____

_____

_____

_____

_____

_____

_____

7. Are you a SEX OFFENDER that is currently required to register by law? Yes_____ No _____

   If your answer is yes, answer the following questions.
   Has your registration been kept current since being required? _____

   If no, explain why not _____

   _____

You must submit your most recent sex offender risk assessment with this application. (This may be obtained from your local sheriff's office.)

App. C, p. 4

8. List all other crimes **not listed before**, even out of state crimes, traffic violations, misdemeanors, etc. **that you do not want to be considered for commutation (time cut)**.

Crime	County of conviction	Date	Court Docket #	Sentence

PERSONAL BACKGROUND

1. Are you: Single _____ Married _____ Separated _____ Divorced _____ Widowed _____

List the following information:

Name of Spouse	Date of marriage	Date Marriage ended	Reason (divorce/death, etc)

App. C, p. 5

2. Do you have children? Yes ____ No ____ If so, how many? _____

Name	Age	Address

3. Have you ever served in the Armed Forces? Yes_____ No _____
   If yes, what branch? _____

4. What type of discharge did you receive? Honorable _____ Dishonorable _____
                                           Medical _____ Other _____

EMPLOYMENT BACKGROUND

1. **Please provide the following information about your current job:**

Name of employer _____

Employer's address and phone #_____

When were you hired_____

Give a brief description of your job duties:

_____

_____

_____

2. If you are currently unemployed, but on disability, please explain how you became disabled.

_____

_____

For previous jobs you have held, list the following information:

Dates From	To	Employer	Address & Current Phone	Reason for Leaving

App. C, p. 6

EDUCATIONAL BACKGROUND

School	Address	Dates of Attendance	Highest grade completed & Degrees

By signing and submitting this application, I hereby swear and affirm that the information provided is true and accurate to the best of my knowledge and I hereby waive any state or federal privacy protections or other privileges to the extent allowable by law.

I understand that incorrect information provided, will be grounds for IMMEDIATE DENIAL!

You must answer all questions or your application will be returned.

Applicant's Signature: _____

Date of Application: _____

Subscribed and sworn to me this _____day of _____, _____.

My Commission expires: _____

_____Notary Public

App. C, p. 7

Appendix D

Instructions

An application for pardon does not guarantee that a pardon will be granted. An applicant for Pardon should understand that the process is lengthy.

The Parole Board must review all applications. After the Parole Board reviews your application and makes its recommendation, you will be notified. Please, do not call the Parole Board concerning results. However, you must notify the Parole Board in the event of an address change.

The Governor relies on the recommendation of the Parole Board and will not review any application that has not been first reviewed by the Parole Board. **The Governor does not review files taken out of order.** There is no appeal process for Pardons. If the Governor denies the application, that decision is final.

Follow all instructions and answer all questions truthfully.

Incorrect information will be grounds for return of your application.

NEW APPLICANTS
If you have never filed a Pardon Application before, attach these certified documents to the application:
1. Judgment and Commitment Order (get from the Circuit Clerks Office if Felony Charge –or– from the District Clerk's office if misdemeanor)
2. Felony Information and/or probable cause affidavit from clerk
3. Narrative incident report from arresting agency (City Police, Sheriff or State Police)
4. If record is sealed, include Order to Seal (get from court clerk)

OLD APPLICANTS
Because you have previously filed for a Pardon, all necessary paperwork is still in your file at the Parole Board. Fill out the application, have it notarized and return it to the Parole Board at the address below. DO NOT resubmit attachments sent before (# 1 – 4 above). Only submit NEW information to support your file.

If you have convictions NOT previously requested, you must furnish the following:
1. Judgment and commitment order
2. Information sheet or probable cause affidavit
3. Narrative incident report from arresting agency (City Police, Sheriff or State Police)

Return all applications to:
DCC Institutional Release Services (IRS)
Pardon Department
2801 S. Olive St., Suite 6-D
Pine Bluff, AR 71603

* If your address or contact information changes for any reason during the application process, please update your information by contacting 870-543-1033.
****

Pardon Application
Institutional Release Services--Pardon Department
2801 S. Olive St., Suite 6-D
Pine Bluff, AR. 71603
870-543-1033 // 870-879-6725 fax

Name _____   Date of Birth _____

Address _____   Race _____ Sex _____

City _____   ADC# _____ PID# _____

State _____ Zip _____   SS# _____

Phone _____   Cell _____

▪▪▪

I am requesting the following (Check Only One)

Option 1: _____ Pardon (with firearm rights restored)
Option 2: _____ Pardon (without firearm rights restored)
Option 3: _____ Restoration of Firearms Only* -- crime must be 8 years old and no weapons involved

*And page **8** also must be filled out by Sheriff in county where you reside and notarized

Checklist for Applicant's Use

Please make sure all information listed below is attached to application

1. _____ First time applicant   Yes _____ No _____
   Date of previous application _____
2. _____ Entirely completed, signed, dated and notarized application
3. _____ Judgment Orders for each conviction to be considered
4. _____ **Letters of recommendation**: (include current address and daytime phone #'s)
   i. Family
   ii. Friends
   iii. Minister (if applicable)
   iv. Present or former employers
   v. Other reputable persons in the community who may desire to testify to the moral character and good behavior of the applicant.
6. _____ Letter of Personal Plea
****

App. D, p. 2   1

1. Give full name under which you were convicted and any alias names you may have used:

_____

_____

2. You must list below, ALL CRIMES FOR WHICH YOU WISH TO BE PARDONED!
(Attach separate sheet if necessary to include all convictions to be considered)

   (fill out completely and attach Judgment OR Commitment Orders (or docket sheets) for each crime listed)

Crime	County of conviction	Date	Court Docket #	Sentence

3. Have you completely discharged from your sentence? YES_____ NO _____
4. Are you on probation or suspended sentence? _____
5. Was any restitution ordered in any of the convictions Yes _____ No _____
6. Have all fines, fees, court costs and restitution been paid in full? If Yes—attach receipts
If you still owe restitution, cost(s) and/or fine(s) for any convictions, please list the persons or entity to which the debt is owed and the outstanding amount still owed.

_____

_____

_____

_____

_____

7. Were there victims in your crimes? YES _____ NO _____
   If yes answer the following questions;
      a. Did you know the victim? _____
      b. If yes, what was the relationship? _____
      c. Was the victim injured? _____
      d. Age of the Victim _____
      e. Was the victim law enforcement or public official? _____
      f. Was there more than one (1) victim? _____
8. Were other persons involved in the crimes listed above? Yes _____ No _____
      If yes, list the names of your accomplices and what, if any, sentences they received

_____

_____

_____

_____

_____

App. D, p. 3

2

9. Concerning the facts of the crimes, briefly explain what happened in each case. (Attach a separate sheet if necessary)

_____

_____

_____

_____

10. Explain the reason why you think the Governor should grant to you the relief requested. (Attach a separate sheet if necessary)

_____

_____

_____

_____

_____

_____

11. Describe what you have done to demonstrate your rehabilitation-Community programs, volunteer work, furthering education, speaking engagements, mentoring to others, etc. (Attach a separate sheet if necessary)

_____

_____

_____

_____

_____

_____

12. Are you a SEX OFFENDER who is currently required to register by law? Yes_____ No _____
    (If your answer is yes, answer the following questions)
    >. Has your registration been kept current since its requirement? _____
    >. If no, explain why not _____

You must submit your most recent risk assessment with this application. This may be obtained from your local sheriff's office)

13. List all other crimes **not listed before**, even out of state crimes, traffic violations, misdemeanors, etc. that you DO NOT WISH TO BE CONSIDERED FOR PARDON

Crime	County of conviction	Date	Court Docket #	Sentence

App. D, p. 4

3

PERSONAL BACKGROUND
▪▪

1. Are you:
Single_____ Married _____ Separated _____ Divorced _____ Widowed _____
Full name of spouse _____
When were you married_____
Where were you married _____

2. Previous marriages: list the following information;
Name of Spouse   Date of Marriage   Date marriage ended   Reason (divorce/death, etc.)
_____
_____
_____
_____
_____
_____

3. Children _____ How many? _____
Name   AGE   Address
_____
_____
_____
_____
_____
_____
_____

4. Have you ever served in the Armed Forces? Yes_____ No _____
   If yes, what branch? _____

5. What type of discharge did you receive? Honorable _____ Dishonorable _____
                                            Medical _____ Other _____

EDUCATIONAL BACKGROUND
▪▪

School	Address	Dates of Attendance	Highest grade completed & Degrees

EMPLOYMENT BACKGROUND

1. Please provide the following information about your current job:

Name of employer _____

Employer's address _____

When were you hired_____

Give a brief description of your job duties:

_____

_____

_____

_____

2. If you are currently unemployed, but on disability, please explain how you became disabled.

_____

_____

_____

_____

For previous jobs you have held, list the following information

Dates		Employer	Address & Current Phone
From	To		

By signing and submitting this application, I hereby swear and affirm that the information provided is true and accurate to the best of my knowledge and I hereby waive any state or federal privacy protections or other privileges to the extent allowable by law;

I understand that incorrect information provided by me will be grounds for IMMEDIATE DENIAL!

_____

Applicant's Signature

_____

Date of Application

Subscribed and sworn to me this _____day of _____, _____

My Commission expires:: _____

_____
Notary Public

App. D, p. 6

5

Certificate to Obtain Information

Ask the Clerk of the Court to fill out this form if he/she is not able to provide you with all the required documents.

I, _____Circuit Clerk or District Clerk of _____County

Have been approached by _____(applicant's name) in an attempt to

obtain a certified copy of his or her commitment orders for the purpose of applying for a

Governor's Pardon. After a good faith effort, a copy of these records cannot be furnished for the

following reason:

_____Case too old, documents have been destroyed

_____A copy has been diligently searched for and cannot be found

_____Court House burned and record was destroyed (year _____)

****

_____
Circuit Clerk/ Deputy Clerk / District Clerk

_____
County Seal

6

This page is required, <u>in addition to the application,</u> if applying for
RESTORATION OF FIREARMS ONLY (Option 3 on Page 1)

This page is <u>NOT</u> required if applying for a pardon.

Recommendation of Chief Law Enforcement Officer in County of Residence

I, _____, hereby recommend

(applicant)_____ for the restoration of his/her right to own or

possess firearms and certify that he/she is of good standing and is deserving of this restoration of

firearm rights. In Accordance with Arkansas Code Annotated § 5-73-103, I confirm that the crime

occurred more than eight (8) years ago and no weapon was involved in the commission of the

crime. This person currently resides at _____which is

within my jurisdiction and has lived within my jurisdiction since _____.

            Sheriff _____

            County of _____

Subscribed and sworn to me this _____day of _____, _____.

_____
                           Notary Public

My commission expires:

_____

Executive Clemency
Arkansas

Applications should not be submitted from probationers or parolees who have not fully discharged their sentence. If there is still probation or parole time left on a sentence, pardons have not typically been granted.

Process:

1. To apply, fill out and return application to Institutional Release Services as listed on the application.*
   > *Please note that inmates must request applications from and return them to their institutional release officer.
2. Include letters of support or recommendation.
3. The Parole Board will place the application on its agenda and make a non-binding recommendation to the Governor.
4. Once the Parole Board makes its recommendation, the Board will notify the applicant and post the results on its website.
5. The Parole Board will forward the full application to the Governor's office approximately 30 days from the listing on the website.
6. Once the application is received in the Governor's office, he has 240 days for consultation, recommendation, and final decision to be made.
7. An appointment may be made with the Governor's Counsel for Clemency and Corrections once the application has reached the Governor's office.
8. The Governor's decision is a final decision.

Outcomes:

There are several possible outcomes when application is made.

1. The Governor may take no action on an application. In this case, the applicant may re-apply on his/her own time frame. The applicant is not barred from re-application for any statutory amount of time.

2. The Governor may deny the application.
   > This will result in three outcomes:
   >> 1. Most applicants will be denied for 4 years from the date of application.
   >> 2. Inmates with a sentence of life in prison without parole will be denied for 6 years from the date of denial.
   >> 3. Inmates with a sentence of life in prison without parole for capital murder will be denied for 8 years from the date of the denial.
   > These are statutorily set denial periods.

3.   The Governor may issue a notice of intent to grant a pardon or commutation. This will trigger a 30 day waiting period for public comment and provide public notice that a clemency action is pending.

>   At the end of the 30 day waiting period, a proclamation may be issued granting the pardon or commutation.
>
>   Issuance of a notice of intent is not an automatic grant. If for any reason, information is received during the 30 day waiting period that is negative, the Governor can choose to not grant the pardon or commutation.

Restoration:

If an applicant is granted a pardon, he or she may have all their rights restored. If the applicant has felony convictions, the pardon may restore the right to bear arms. If the applicant has a misdemeanor conviction, with the exception of domestic battery convictions, there was never a loss of the second amendment rights.

If an applicant is granted a commutation, the time required to be served in the Department of Correction will be shortened. This is not a full pardon and does not restore rights that have been lost. For full restoration, a full pardon must be asked for at a future date.

Contact with the Governor's office:

Jenny Wilkinson
Counsel for Clemency and Corrections
State Capitol Room 011
Little Rock, AR 72201
501-683-6447

Made in the USA
Coppell, TX
31 July 2022

80667882R10059